Practical Gardening on the Costa

Published by BLANCA BOOKS, S.L.
Apartado 95,
03500 Benidorm,
(Alicante),
Spain

Published September 2001
Reprinted November 2002
Reprinted August 2004

Copyright ©2001 of text, the authors Clodagh and Richard Handscombe
Copyright ©2001 of book, CB News S.L.

All rights reserved. No part of this publication may be reproduced or transmitted, in any form or by any means, without permission in writing from the authors and publishers.

The book 'Practical Gardening on the Costa' is available through newsagents, book shops and by mail order direct through CB News S.L.

Design and typesetting by Theresa Marín.

Printed and bound in Spain by Artes Gráficas Esquerdo, Part. Torres 9, Villajoyosa (Alicante)

Depósito Legal: A-1105-2001   ISBN: 84-607-2827-7

PRACTICAL GARDENING ON THE COSTA
- Your Personal Guide

*Clodagh and Dick
alias Greenfingers*

CB News S.L. Spain

Contents

Preface

Section A. Designing and improving gardens

1. The Spanish gardening challenge.
2. Review of an established garden.
3. Starting a new garden.
4. Rediscovering an overgrown garden.
5. Design of small gardens.
6. The importance of shade.
7. Creating gardens in pine trees.
8. A children's corner.
9. The challenge facing the absentee gardener.
10. Design for elderly, disabled and infirm.

Section B. Creating and maintaining a flower garden

11. The flower garden in January/February.
12. The flower garden in March/April.
13. The flower garden in May/June.
14. The flower garden in July/August.
15. The flower garden in September/October.
16. The flower garden in November/December.
17. Propagation.
18. Gazanias.
19. Geraniums.
20. Lantanas.
21. Oleanders.
22. Succulent terrace pots.
23. Spectacular flowering plants.
24. Climbing plants.
25. Colour matching plants.
26. Petunias, busy lizzies and fuchsias.
27. Summer annuals.
28. Sweet peas.
29. Establishing a herb garden.
30. Perfume in the garden.
31. Roses, selection and planting.
32. Roses, planting and first year care.
33. Roses, care of mature plants and propagation.
34. Camelias.
35. Flowering trees.
36. Palms.
37. Cacti.
38. Hedges - boundary and internal.
39. Establishing wildlife in the garden.
40. Attracting butterflies.
41. Establishing a wilderness corner.
42. Garden bulbs.
43. Garden pond - construction.
44. Garden pond - stocking.
45. Constructing a rockery.
46. Review of garden furniture and ornaments.
47. Christmas plants - purchasing.
48. Christmas plants - aftercare.

Section C. Creating and maintaining a vegetable garden

49. The vegetable garden in February/March.
50. The vegetable garden in April/May.
51. The vegetable garden in June/July.
52. The vegetable garden in August/September.
53. The vegetable garden in October/November.
54. The vegetable garden in December/January.
55. Plant protection in the vegetable garden.
56. Comfrey - an invaluable herb.
57. Organic gardening - definition and benefits.
58. Annual vegetable garden review.
59. Companion planting and lunar calendar.
60. Crop rotation.
61. Soil testing and improvement.
62. Control of snails.
63. Tomatoes.
64. Onions, leeks and garlic.
65. Marrow and squashes.
66. Asparagus.
67. Brassicas.
68. Spaghetti.

Section D. Creating and maintaining a fruit garden

69. Melons.
70. Establishing an orchard.
71. Establishing a soft fruit patch.
72. Grapevines.
73. Citrus fruits.
74. Cash crop trees.
75. Pruning of fruit trees.

Section E. General issues

76. Natural feeds and sprays.
77. Waterless gardening.
78. Maximising water retention.
79. Installation and improvement of watering systems.
80. Adding a greenhouse and garden frame.
81. Garden safety.
82. Practical gardening tools.
83. Establishing a compost heap.
84. Bonfires.
85. Twenty jobs for a rainy day.
86. Garden planning chart.
87. Garden expenditure record.

Section F. Readers support

88. Summary of Word Corners.
89. Useful English/Spanish questions and possible answers.
90. Readers request page.

Acknowledgements.
Index.
Personal notes for action.

Dedication

To gardeners with the courage and patience to conquer the climate of the Costas

Preface

Gardening is probably the most popular outdoor activity enjoyed by people like us. People who have purchased permanent or holiday homes on the Costa. This book is written for them as a personal guide for developing attractive and productive gardens. A book to be used.

All of us find gardening on the Costa very different to what we experienced before, largely in Northern Europe. When we first came to the area we found, like most, that published advice specific to the coastal and inland microclimate of the Costas was sparse, and in insufficient detail. This book is designed to take much of the pain out of your initial and ongoing learning process. Whether starting from scratch or improving an existing garden, we share our first hand "how to do it" experience. Practical experience gained creating our own gardens from nothing and advising others in a wide range of situations over the last 15 years. By taking good and sometimes bad advice and by continuous experimentation we have managed to marshal many of the skills necessary to create attractive and productive flower, vegetable and fruit gardens, where soil and water allow.

Two years ago we were delighted to accept the invitation to write the weekly Practical Gardening column in CB News under the pseudonym Greenfingers. Since then we have written in a practical way about a wide range of topics. Topics that were important to us, friends and those readers who wrote in with their personal gardening problems.

The response to our writing has been great. We have been especially encouraged by visible signs that our ideas are being put into practice, with success. The publication of the book "Practical Gardening on the Costa" was a natural follow-on. The book is a collection of 85 columns that have appeared in the CB News. The columns, now chapters, have been collated into six sections colour coded for ease of access. They are:

A. Designing and improving gardens:
B: Creating and maintaining a flower garden
C. Creating and maintaining a vegetable garden
D. Creating and maintaining a fruit garden
E. General issues
F. Reader support

Each chapter contains practical advice and ideas. They include easy to follow check lists and questionnaires where appropriate. Most chapters are illustrated by photographs. Photographs of what can be achieved by enthusiastic amateur gardeners with the interest and dedication to accept the Spanish Gardening Challenge, the topic of Chapter 1.

To help you find your way through the book the contents list is supported by a comprehensive crossreferencing index. Naturally some topics such as planting, feeding and controlling pests are covered in a number of chapters.

The weekly English-Spanish Word Corners of the past two years are summarised at the back of the book. Some useful English-Spanish questions have been added. You will also find useful garden planning and record charts, space for personal notes and a readers' request page. Problems sent in will continue to be dealt with in future Practical Gardening columns in the Costa Blanca News and Costa del Sol News for the benefit of all.

We hope that this practical book and follow-on columns help readers shape the future of gardening on the Costa. The end result being better gardens, with less effort and expenditure but much enjoyment.

Clodagh and Dick

1. The Spanish Gardening Challenge

If we had a never ending supply of good inexpensive water we would probably all have amazing gardens.

At their best Spanish gardens are dramatic and productive. Profusely flowering, aromatic and yielding fruit and vegetables every month of the year. Personal havens in which to enjoy gardening and relaxation. But at their worst they are parched, flowerless deserts. Wherever you are on the Spanish coast you will see evidence of both. Perhaps even as neighbouring gardens. The challenge is very obvious.

If you want to enjoy outdoor living in pleasant surroundings why not take up the challenge?

The start point is to understand the pluses and minuses of gardening on the Mediterranean coast. Once understood the challenge is not as daunting as it may seem at first sight.

THE POSITIVE SIDE

- The climate allows us to garden for more than 300 days a year. 300 days for the procreation of plants, flowers and fruit.

- Gardening is good exercise. As one ages the heavier jobs can be delegated to a professional gardener.

- Plants can flower and fruit every day of the year. There is an abundance of interesting native and naturalised plants that are reasonably drought resistant and generally value for money. And as a bonus the hot climate makes propagation easy. Painting with flowers becomes a reality.

- Once established most perennials, bulbs, shrubs and trees do not need constant care and attention. Mainly an annual winter cut back. The exception is annuals that need constant watering.

- The climate allows us to be outside for long hours throughout the year, not only for gardening, but also for working, dining, partying and siestas.

- Where in the world can you eat in the garden with so few insects bothering you on a balmy summer's night?

- Colourful terraces and nayas become a part of the garden rather than extensions to the house.

THE NEGATIVE SIDE

- Many gardens have impoverished soil. Rocky, stony, sandy or clay and often starved of humus and essential nutrients. At least compared with our previous gardening experiences. Naturally some people are fortunate in purchasing a house built on what was productive agricultural land.

- Many houses have a shortage rather than an abundance of water - the result of 300 days sunshine rather than 300 days of rain. Many years produce little and infrequent rainfall. In some years spring showers and even the autumn 'gota fria' fail to materialise. In some towns wells run dry or turn salty, especially in the summer. A small minority of gardens are fed by an ancient supply of abundant sweet agricultural water.

- Top soil can be shallow, only a few centimetres rather than metres deep above bed rock and between outcrops of rock. But such situations can be turned into wonderful rockeries without the import of scarce and expensive topsoil.

Against this background there are 10 basic rules for grasping and achieving the challenge.

1. Design and develop your garden to live in.
2. Plant mainly native and naturalised plants.
3. Respect water shortages. Only water when essential.
4. Enrich soils ecologically and increase water retention.
5. Plant closely to shade roots.
6. Use natural terrain and features to create interest.
7. Preserve and plant mature trees for shade. Spain provides the sun.
8. Maximise terraces and paths. Minimise lawns.
9. Do the annual clean up in January rather than in October.
10. Have a long-term vision of the garden. Reflect each year on the successes and failures. Above all focus on your future. You will hopefully live in and enjoy your garden for the rest of your life.

2. Review of an established garden

Many gardeners realise that there is always room for improvement in their gardens, even when mature.

The autumn is a good time to commence making changes. The weather is cooler for heavy work and the soil more workable if we have had recent rain. However, before deciding what to change, what to move and what to add, it is worth reflecting on:

- the successes and failures in the flower garden during the past spring and summer and
- what is anticipated for the autumn and winter.

Divide your garden into areas, e.g. front garden, side garden A+B, back garden, pool area, terrace and naya.

Then sit and look at the garden from various positions and ask yourself the following questions area by area. Make notes as you progress round the garden during a morning or over several days. Do the review alone or with your spouse or partner.

1. Have we been happy with the general appearance and impact of the area?

2. Did we achieve a continuous show of colour from flowers and blossom?

3. Do we have enough contrasts between the leaves, shapes and heights of the different flowering plants, shrubs and trees?

4. Did flowers and leaves create sufficient daytime and eveningtime perfume as we sat or strolled in the garden?

5. Did we make the best use of planted or empty pots?

6. If we planted annuals were they worth the effort or should we replace them with perennials succulents or shrubs?

7. Did we use too much water in keeping plants alive during the long spring and summer drought? Should we change or add a watering system? Should we install a watering system computer?

8. Do we now have good early autumn colour and can we expect it to last through to the end of the year?

9. Can we make the best use of the winter sun?

10. Did we have sufficient shade in the garden? Were the shady areas interesting and restful?

11. What were the focal points in the garden, in addition to the pool if you have one?

12. Are the plants, trees, lawn, paths and walls in good condition?

13. Which areas required a lot of maintenance? What can we do to reduce this for next year?

14. Did each area phase and blend into adjacent areas in a harmonious manner?

15. Did we have good, colourful views from each doorway and window?

16. If one or two areas were real eye catchers ask yourself - How can we achieve a similar effect in another area or corner of the garden?

Then reflect on your findings. Decide on the priorities for improvements and when best to make them.
It is amazing how the gardening year soon passes. Naturally most plantings and the heaviest jobs are best done from November to March.
We suggest you carry out a similar review each autumn or spring.

3. Starting a new garden

Many new owners face the major challenge of creating gardens in a climate and soil of which they have no prior experience. Each with their own objectives for their flower garden, vegetable plot and orchard.

Naturally garden size and terrain vary and are major determinants of what is possible, as are the ages of home buyers. However five factors are common to all.

Firstly most new homes are being built on land that was previously one of the following:
a. Dry semi-desert coastal land.
b. Natural hillside and pinewoods.
c. Terraces uncultivated for decades. Olive and almond trees having died due to lack of rainfall.
d. Agricultural land on which orange trees, almond trees and vegetables still survive or have died due to salt water contaminating the land. Few will be lucky enough to have a new house built on good agricultural land - this is still regarded too precious for development.

The start point is therefore potentially hostile. But with care, hard work and perseverance fantastic gardens will develop within a few years. Of course, if one has the money, the easy solution is to use a landscaper who will move in a metre or more of topsoil, plant an instant garden with mature trees and shrubs, kept alive by a complex computer-controlled watering system... at a price!

Secondly, water is becoming more expensive and not available in many areas in sufficient quantity or quality to maintain large lawns and thirsty plants. The best solution is to base the main garden design around non thirsty plants that are natural to Spain.

Thirdly, it is important to do as much as possible to improve the soil so that it absorbs and retains water at natural root depths, i.e. five to 50cm below soil level.

Fourthly, it is important to prevent surface evaporation and the drying out of the top 15cms by covering the soil between plants with mulch, rocks, paths, rock chippings over plastic sheets, pools and ponds.

Fifthly, many buyers will have more time for gardening now than during their working lives. Bearing the above in mind we suggest the following 10 tasks for the first six months for the new garden owner. The garden starting out as a dry, rocky, weedy plot decorated by rubble left by the builder.

1. Prepare a site plan. Mark up the boundaries and house to scale but no more at this stage. These are the only unchangeables. Don't rush into an immediate garden design. Think about the possibilities for a while. First complete tasks two and three.

2. Survey your plot and identify:
- vistas to be retained and enhanced.
- natural features such as mature trees, old terrace walls, large rocks, hollows, old walls etc., worth preserving as key features.
- pockets of good, deep soil.
- areas of shallow soil over bedrock.
- naturally damper areas as a result of slope and surrounding bed rock.

Identify where weeds grow most luxuriantly. This is where shrubs will grow best in the future. Also identify where little or nothing grew naturally. This is where plants will struggle to survive in the future. Obvious? Yes but we still see lawns and thirsty plants planted in 10 to 20cms of soil over the top of the septic tank. It would be better covered with a terrace!

As you explore the plot mark up the information you gather on your site plan.

3. Wander around your new neighbourhood and public gardens in local towns. Make a note of what plants look attractive and luxuriant in various situations and just as important what seems to struggle and look dry and untidy.

4. Start to visualise a few garden layouts. Take several copies of your site plan with gathered information and start to sketch them out. Have vision. Check their basic viability against the information you have recorded from your investigatory tour of the plot.

5. Clear the plot of builder's rubble and loose rocks. Place them in graded piles. All can probably be utilised or lost in constructing paths, terraces, walls or rockeries.

6. Clear away the weeds.
a. If you have a small, rocky plot do this by hand using a mattock - a tool which all Spaniards use - it is nearly impossible to use a fork or spade when the ground is so hard. Stack the weeds in a suitable position for a compost heap.
b. If you have a large plot arrange for it to be ploughed or rotavated except where you expect to construct terraces. You will need a firm base.
c. As an alternative to a and b place the dug/hoed weeds on areas for prime planting. Add a layer of manure and cover with carpet or plastic. This will produce a rich soil for later planting.

7. **Decide on and plant hedges.** Water the plants in well and regularly or put in a drip system until established.

8. **Decide on where to have terraces.** Mark them out with posts and string, lines of stone or with large sheets of plastic cut to shape and weighted down with stones or gravel. The latter allows one to experiment with a number of positions and shapes. Also plastic can be speedily covered with attractive stone chippings. The chippings can be used as the final surface or as the foundation for slabs at a later date.

9. Decide where you want to have more shade. Select and plant attractive flowering trees or olives, carobs or palms. Support all trees with strong stakes until well established. Once established these will not need too much water.

10. Decide on where your main flowerbeds will be. Also the vegetable plot if you plan one. You have two options. Start to plant immediately or enrich the soil for three to 12 months. We prefer the latter. Most planting can then be done during the winter months.

4. Rediscovering an overgrown garden

Many of us have purchased properties in Spain with long neglected established gardens, best described as overgrown or wildernesses!

Gardens in which for example -

1. None of the plants have been pruned properly since it was first laid out some years before.
2. Some plants have become very stunted or have died due to the shortage of water.
3. Weeds have overtaken cultivated plants.
4. Nothing has been fed.
5. Rampant plants have smothered lower growing plants. All intermingled as in a jungle.

Naturally if you are new to Spain, having lived your previous life in the UK or other northern European countries, your experience to date has been of a verdant green garden. A garden with a perfect lawn, rose beds, formal shrub beds and a mass of summer annuals. All watered weekly by several days of rain. Very different to your new gardening challenge. You probably know nothing about Mediterranean gardening. You would like a nice garden but don't want to spend all your time bashing away in the heat.

So where to start?

The following are our practical suggestions for the first six months.

a. First of all take your time and go through the garden methodically.

b. If you have to have a gardener beware. Many will not investigate what is worth saving. They may come in and chop and clear. There are probably many good plants within and underneath the jungle.

c. If there are signs of flowerbeds go through them carefully weeding as you go and pruning each plant back to shape. The best time to clean a garden is from October to March or even up to May, as all plants will benefit from a good pruning. In the heat of the summer plants should be treated less harshly.

d. Once the flowerbeds have been cleaned up things will start taking shape. If for example you have cleaned up between October and March wait until the following October before you are tempted to buy more than a few plants. Over the summer you will have had a chance to see exactly how the plants recover and flower.

e. The plants you are most likely to find will be plants which are most commonly grown here. They will require little attention if mature. They are reasonably drought tolerant. For instance:

- Margaritas which come in many colours. Prune them back quite hard.
- Herbs such as rosemary, lavender and sage - give them a hard trim
- Gazanias - low growing in many colours. Clumps will need tidying up and perhaps splitting.
- Lantana - this is a very colourful long-flowering plant which comes in several colours. If leggy they should be pruned back to the main stump. They soon recover strongly. They often give you continuous colour throughout 10 months of the year.
- Geraniums - if not diseased, cut them back hard. Pot up the strongest cuttings.

f. Climbers have often got into a real mess smothering other plants, pergolas and even the house. Deal with them one at a time. Prune bougainvilleas back hard along the lateral branches. Take out suckers recognised by the straight lighter green stems and larger leaves. Bignonias can grow rampant. Leave in whatever branches you want and cut off all the side shoots. Plumbago and jasmine need to be cut back to shape.

g. If there are fruit trees that have been neglected they will need a good pruning. It might be a good idea to get a local Spaniard to prune them for you the first time. If you don't want to spend too much time on the orchard initially just make a well around the base of the trees and flood them monthly. Perhaps hire a strimmer to clean up all around. If the trees are diseased you can always ask for advice in your local Co-operativa Agricola or horticultural shop. Take a friend who speaks some Spanish.

h. Yuccas are a popular plant but with very sharp points. Especially if there are going to be children in the garden you should cut off the sharp tips. To tidy up lower leaves pull them off leaving a nice smooth trunk.

i. You may find that cacti have multiplied. Retain only plants that have a good shape and are in a sensible place.

j. You may have palms which urgently need cutting back. If you don't want the expense of getting them professionally cut, they are easy to deal with. Provided they aren't too tall.

Here are a few tips -

1. Buy a good curved pruning saw. The proper tool makes life much easier
2. When cutting be very careful of the sharp points nearest the trunk. They are lethal. It is a good idea to cut off those sharp tips first.

If you have a lot of rubbish pile it up near to the entrance. When you have finished the clean-up hire a skip to take it away, or alternatively use a shredder to shred everything. Most prunings can be shredded except stringy things like palm fronds, cacti etc. The shredded waste is useful on your kitchen compost heap or as mulch in the garden.

We hope that these ideas will help you discover and save what is already in the garden. You will have made a useful start and can now sit back and think about garden improvements for the autumn.

5. *Design of small gardens*

Not everyone has a 1,000 or 2,000 square metre plot or more. Some houses are on a plot of only 500 to 600 square metres. Allowing 120 square metres for the house, this leaves only 380 to 480 square metres for a garden. And this includes the car area and terraces. The design of such gardens needs special care if an intimate, attractive environment is to be achieved. A garden that looks good and is a pleasure to be in, in all seasons. You do not need a big garden to achieve this.

The following guidelines should help you achieve a garden that is unique to your property, location, needs and personality. They can be used in starting a new garden from scratch or revamping an existing one. We suggest you first use the guidelines to prepare an outline plan on paper before taking out the spade.

1. Aim to create an enclosed haven for your family and visiting wildlife. A garden that supports your planned life style.

2. Create a solid/semi-solid screen around the plot to provide privacy, and protection and support for boundary plants. You may be lucky enough to have a walled garden. If not, which will be in most cases, construct a two-metre wire mesh fence and line it with rolled fencing. Those made from reeds, canes and bushy cuttings can all look attractive to yourself and neighbours. If you live in an urbanisation, check out local bylaws.

3. Dig a two-metre wide and metre deep trench on the inside of the boundary wall or fence. If the soil is good, mix it 2:1 with well-rotted compost or manure and refill the trench. If the soil is poor or full of rubble etc., put it aside for going under a raised terrace or have it removed to a local approved tip.

4. Are there any things beyond the fence that you want to

A rough beginning

Two years later

block out? For instance the windows of the next door house, an unsightly pylon, or a view of the motorway. Select and plant maturing trees that will block out the offending vista within just a few years. Choose trees such as olives and mimosa that can easily be kept to a maximum height of three or four metres. This should achieve your objectives without offending the neighbours.

5. Plant a conifer or adelfas hedge half a metre from the wire mesh fence or a mix of climbers, preferably evergreen against a wall. These will settle and will start to spread while you deal with the rest of the garden. Plant a white jasmine near the gate to give a perfumed entry. Something many Spanish gardens have.

6. Dig a similar trench around the house and fill likewise with good soil.

7. Select and plant a range of climbers such as bougainvilleas, honeysuckle, roses, passionflower, wisteria and plumbago to create the beginning of a multicoloured display in the first year. Be sure to include a dama de noche for its night-time perfume.

8. Decide on where you want to have terraces for eating out, Jacuzzi, sunbathing, swing, clothes drying and dustbins. Double the sizes you first thought of. You will always have guests to accommodate, clothes blow out in the wind and one always needs a storage/work area for the wheelbarrow, logs, potting, compost heap, etc. The edges of the terraces can obviously overlap the dug areas around the house and fence. The good soil and the cover of the terrace can provide a fertile damp area for spreading damp roots. This will help reduce summer watering.

9. Next decide on the type of surface that would look good. The possibilities include:

- Concrete - bland and uninteresting, even if coloured.
- Flat broken rock slabs set in concrete. Firm, non-slip and look good with an attractive texture and colour.
- Terracotta tiles in a variety of sizes.
- Herringbone or other designs of concrete blocks laid in sand or concrete. Tends to look suburban if cheap brick is used.
- Broken paving slabs. Not as easy to get as in Northern Europe and often not a very pleasant effect. Decide whether the car driveway should be in the same material.

10. Decide how the front, back and French doors are to be interconnected to each other and the various terrace areas. Again decide on materials. You could use the same as the terraces or contrasting stone chippings or old railway sleepers for instance. The advantage of rock chippings and rock slabs is that you can lay down paths as a trial. Then reflect on the impact for a few weeks before making permanent or modifying to achieve a more pleasing effect. Lay rock chippings on plastic to prevent weeds, and rock slabs on cement to achieve a stable path without weeds.

11. Decide on where you need shade. Select and plant a number of fast-maturing, medium-height trees such as, mimosa, apricot, almond. Each of these will add colour with flowers in the spring.

12. Now decide on the extent and shape of flower/shrub beds around the paths and around the house and along the borders. Mark them out with posts and string. Test out a number of options before finalising.

13. You will now be left with a number of irregular shaped unused areas of earth. Decide whether you really want straight lines or would rounded shapes not look more attractive and add a sense of space?

14. Then decide on the best surface on the remaining areas. Options include:

Grass - but do you want the hassle and expense of establishing and maintaining a pristine lawn in a dry climate with increasing water restrictions in the summer?

Small rock chippings laid over plastic to prevent weeds from growing. Provided a small size and attractive colour is chosen they can give a pleasant effect, offset plants and are easy to maintain.

15. The basic framework is now complete. You can now plant the front of the beds around the house, the boundary and terraces with a range of interesting plants and shrubs. It is your choice whether you want to recreate the garden you had before coming to Spain or experiment with the creation of a Mediterranean garden.

Start by filling in with plants that establish themselves quickly, give colour for many months and perfume the garden in the evening.

For a start consider lantanas, heathers, rosemary, thyme, sage, rockroses, margaritas, gazanias, succulents and cacti.

16. Each spring and autumn, review the garden. Modify its design and content until you have a haven in which you can relax for the rest of your days.

6. *The importance of shade*

It is hot here, and shade is important in all our gardens. But shade has to be developed, sun is always available. In the garden review questionnaire of Chapter 2, one question is:- "Is there sufficient colourful shade in the summer?" Talking to friends we find that the answer in many cases is no. If we are lucky we will have inherited a specimen tree or two. Large spreading trees with sufficient shade to eat, siesta, read or play in on a hot spring or summer day. The mature trees may have been planted originally for a cash crop or may be one of the spectacular flowering trees that thrive in the Spanish climate and soils. Trees that originally generated seasonal crops include the carob, fig, oak, olive, almond, mulberry, apricot, cherry and nut producing pine trees. Then there are flowering trees. The most common being the jacaranda, mimosas, tamarisk, and schinus (pepper tree), each can be spectacular when mature. They can provide up to 20-30 metres of usable shade or more. Sadly year by year mountainsides become deforested and the stock of mature trees in residential areas is also on the decline. Mature specimen trees are being cut down monthly. Firstly by developers wanting a clear plot before building. Often they have little regard for the environment or imagination of what a mature tree could add to the eventual owner's garden or the impact on garden wildlife. Secondly by purchasers of existing houses. Often mature trees are cut down to improve the lawn, to remove the work of raking or sweeping up fallen leaves or fruit, or to improve the view. The last reason often adds to the total impact of the garden but a heavy pruning may have had the same effect and saved the tree and shade. Before cutting down any more specimens consider the potential benefit to yourselves if summer residents, or to your summer tenants if the house is let. If you have not done so already review your own garden, the following questions and ideas may help you. Do we have good shade other than on the north side of the house? Have we only large trees round the boundary with none in the central area? Do we want to achieve an oasis, field or desert effect? Should we consider planting one or two trees this month or in the autumn?

Before purchasing new trees first wander round a few garden centres, public gardens and friends' gardens. Consider the colour of foliage and flowers and the shadow given by young and mature trees. Check with the garden centre whether their trees have been prepared for spring or autumn planting. Large trees can only be planted bare root in the winter or early spring. They are best planted from large containers.

Have we made best use of the available shade by creating sizeable terraces or cosy corners?

Eating terraces need 20 square metres for a table and six chairs. Cosy corners can be as small as four square metres. Just enough to have a quiet siesta, or read, and these days for the inevitable mobile phone. We predict it won't be long before an enterprising person markets the garden phone booth - it could double up as a small greenhouse!

Have we used a terrace material that looks good, wears well and is easy to keep under trees?

Stone slabs and stone chippings are generally more successful than terracotta tiles or lawn. Have we planted colourful shrubs, ground cover plants and bulbs at the edge of or in the depth of the shade?

Shady terraces can be dull without colour. Consider the following general design as a start point for your own ideas.

1. In the semi-shade near the trunk a circle or semi-circle of pots with geraniums, margaritas, fuchsias, amaryllis, or clivias.

2. Create a circular or oval bed around the outer edge of the shadow of the tree going out into the sun. Plant lantanas, hibiscus, hollyhocks, margaritas, gazanias, lilies or agapanthus. Also consider planting a climber such as a passionflower, wisteria or bignonia and train it up through the outer branches to flower above the upper leaves. This can look spectacular.

3. Lastly does our garden furniture blend in? Should we make a change in the style, construction, material or colour? White plastic seats and tables often look out of place except by the pool. However they can be easily painted in a green or brown tint that blends in with the surrounding trees and plants. A thorough review of garden furniture and ornaments is considered in Chapter 46.

7. Creating gardens in pine trees

Many new developments have been, and still are, being built on land that was previously unspoilt pinewood or copse.

By careful planning and taking a few precautions, interesting gardens can be created. Gardens that take advantage of the natural semi-shaded glades and acid soil.

But all too often the commercial developers of individual homes and estates start by felling most or all of the trees, often removing or burying the valuable topsoil and spreading building rubble across the site. There is an immediate irreversible environmental loss for the eventual occupiers and neighbours.

1. A valuable natural habitat for permanent and migratory birds has disappeared. We have recently lost woods on two sides of our house. Luckily our own trees screen the newly built houses. Many common birds have made their homes in our bird-friendly garden. But the more rare species that sheltered in the woods will probably not return. This includes the golden orioles, tree creepers and eagle owls.

2. The loss of a natural habitat for wild and cultivated plants and trees that enjoy an acid semi-shaded microclimate.

3. A change in the natural water table. The original pine trees will not be sucking up water. But more importantly the original shade and thick underlay of composting pine trees is no longer retaining moisture and preventing evaporation. The soil therefore dries out quickly and newly planted plants require expensive watering. When storms come much water runs off the plot. At worst serious soil erosion occurs and newly planted plants get washed out.

But it need not be so if you are prepared for some hard work and regular clearing up of pine needles. We offer the following guidelines:

1. Purchase a plot with healthy pine trees.

2. Position the house in an area of least density of trees and persuade the architect and builder to only cut down the rogue, diseased trees and the minimum required for a driveway, the house and to provide strategically-placed glades and terraces.

3. Develop a house design that maximises the outlook on interesting vistas from windows, doorways and terraces.

4. Before developing a detailed garden, visit and walk through a number of new and mature pinewoods. Make a note of the plants that survive and struggle and typical natural features.

a. on the edge of the woods
b. alongside pathways
c. in partial shade
d. in full shade
e. in glades
f. on banks and terraces
g. in hollows and barrancos
h. around a natural pool or spring

Decide on the type of features and effects that you would like to retain or create.

5. Check on the depth and quality of soil. Pine trees can grow on a shallow soil covering of rocks. Many plants will not grow in this shallow acid soil. You may therefore need to import soil to create one-metre deep beds behind rock walls before commencing to plant. Plants can also be potted in large pots.

Consider the following plants and trees when ready to develop a detailed plan and starting to plant up.

Recognise that very few plants will grow well in the darkness of a dense wood. Plants need at least filtered sun for part of the day. Sunny sheltered glades can be very colourful.

1. ALONGSIDE THE DRIVEWAY

The following possibilities immediately come to mind. They can be integrated to achieve colour all year round.

a. a line of heathers and/or herbs such as rosemary, lavender, thyme, sage and rue
b. a line of yellow broom or clipped gorse
c. a line of irises
d. a line of lilies - dramatic but costly
e. a line of large cacti
f. our favourite - a line of orange/red lantana. These can provide a colourful entrance from May to January. They will benefit from a hard winter cutback.

2. IN THE WOODLAND GLADES

Within the woodland areas plant a mixture of woodland plants and bulbs that thrive in semi-shaded glades. Not much will grow if no light comes through. There are many possibilities

a. large pots of petunias and busy lizzies
b. heathers
c. strong growing herbs, such as rosemary, lavender, thyme and sage
d. trees that add interest such as decorative cypresses, Spanish oaks and the strawberry tree

e. flowering shrubs, such as camellias, rock roses, oleanders, viburnum and perhaps even a magnolia
f. where sun shines on trunks, plant climbers such as variegated ivies, honeysuckles, wisteria and passionflowers.
g. a variety of succulents or cacti in groups between rocks
h. the soft pointed yuccas
i. forest fruits that could be planted include a cultivated blackberry to replace wild ones, a loganberry or raspberry canes especially if your site is in a high inland valley. Also why not plant woodland strawberries? Before planting fruits clear the top layers of dry and well-rotted pine needles to uncover the underlying soil. Dig in well-rotted manure, plant the plants and then mulch with well-rotted manure. Surround with black plastic to retain moisture and keep weed free and cover with stone chippings, old pine needles etc., to hide the plastic.
j. if you like mushrooms, consider seeding an area with seta spawn. But be sure you can identify which are edible and which are poisonous. We could not, so we wouldn't risk it.

3. ALONGSIDE A BARRANCO OR BOUNDARY WALL

Consider planting large, naturally occurring cacti. They grow into spectacular specimens and in time can provide an impenetrable hedge.

4. A NATURAL POOL

Make a special feature of an existing or specially built pond, using a plastic liner. Reeds, bulrushes, irises and other bog plants will soon naturalise to create an interesting feature and natural habitat for frogs and toads.

5. A VEGETABLE CLEARING

Lastly, consider removing a few trees to create an open, semi-shaded glade in which to grow a variety of vegetables. A plot of only 8 x 15 metres, well-manured and watered and closely planted can yield useful quantities of potatoes, beans, peas, lettuces, tomatoes etc.

We hope that the above ideas save a few pine copses as well as creating interesting gardens. But do recognise the risks.

- Pine trees survive in dry conditions but they are thirsty trees. Their roots spread a long way searching for moisture. So a watering system may be essential at least for the first few years until plants are established.
- A layer of pine needles can suffocate plants. Therefore, do a regular picking up and raking. A garden hoover/blower can be very useful.
- Pines can become unstable in gale force winds. Check for any movement of root balls after storms and high winds.
- Pine trees are susceptible to wood-eating beetle and fungi attacks. If trees begin to look sick seek professional advice. If dangerous lop before they do serious damage.
- Pine trees and dry undergrowth are always a fire hazard. As a precaution, cut off branches to three metres above the ground and clear out wild undergrowth. Put up no smoking signs and ensure that you have a hose that reaches to the edge of the property. Also purchase fire brooms and place visibly in strategic parts of the garden.

8. *A children's corner*

Many gardens will be full of young children during the summer, not always so welcome by the end of the summer! A pool is a big attraction but day after day of hot sun can have its toll. Sunburnt irritable children need more to occupy them. There is more than the telly, and it is best to divert them from football in flowerbeds and hide and seek in valuable shrub beds.

The following list is suggested as a start point:

1. A sandpit away from the pool in the shade.

2. An exercise area, swing and climbing frame.

3. A tree house in a specimen tree, on strong, safe branches near to the trunk.

4. A small hut as a den, probably more robust and cooler than a tent; even better if installed with a computer terminal.

5. Pitch and putt or croquet on the lawn.

6. A badminton net. Children manage this easier than tennis.

7. A mini table tennis table.

8. A basket ball net now seems popular with all ages.

9. Own secluded eating terrace, near house for ease of serving and supervision.

10. Own pot plants to tend.

11. Children's garden. Planting and tending sunflowers, pumpkins, gourds, radishes and lettuces can be time consuming and educational.

12. A nature table on which treasures found in the garden, on the sea shore and in the countryside can be displayed.

13. A small library of garden and nature-related books. They may sow the seeds for the next generation of gardeners to come.

We hope these ideas help you have a pleasant and peaceful summer.

9. The challenge facing the absentee gardener

You have become an absentee gardener like many before. Recently you purchased your new Spanish holiday home. It is probably on a rough site or with an unexciting garden.

You plan to visit only one month to five months a year. Like many absentee gardeners you wish to:
- *Have a colourful garden whenever you visit.*
- *Not let out your home.*
- *Minimise the cost of watering during your absence.*
- *Either not employ a gardener, or only for a few hours a month.*
- *Enjoy creating a garden yourself when in Spain.*

You face a major challenge which many have experienced in the past, including ourselves and neighbours.

We suggest the following practical guidelines.

1. Decide on the times of the year when you are likely to visit your Spanish home.

2. Develop a vision of your long-term garden and a development plan for the first few years. Don't rush to complete overnight.

3. Start to plant up the garden area by area with plants that need little attention and little watering once established except for a major winter cutback in January/February. Firstly cacti, succulents and yuccas. They provide interest and the occasional flowers and require little water. Palms also add interest but they will need watering for the first few years. Secondly flowering plants and trees. But recognise they will need more care and attention and watering.

4. Plant plants that are likely to flower or fruit around the times of your most regular visits. What are the possibilities? We suggest the following:

We have indicated probable best flowering times. However, these obviously depend on weather conditions, watering and feeding and the actual location of your home. The needs of each plant are covered in more detail in later chapters.

To achieve the above flowering patterns carry out the winter pruning in January and not in October/November which is normal in Northern Europe.

To have instant colour when you are here for only a few weeks why not buy annuals such as petunias, pansies, busy lizzies etc., which come in many colours. There is a huge selection available all the year round from garden centres and flower shops. In the hotter months you must be prepared to water them daily. An idea for absentee gardeners is to keep the plants in the original pots when planting in beds and terrace pots. When you go, instead of leaving them to die in the heat, take them out and pass on to resident neighbours and friends.

5. It will be important to take special care with new plantings. We find that the best months are October and March. Plant plants in large holes filled with soil enriched by moisture-retaining compost or well-rotted manure. Plant through black plastic sheeting. After planting cover the plastic sheeting with stone chippings or a thin layer of soil. The soil under the plastic will remain damp and weeds will be suppressed. If you don't use plastic, plant plants close together so that they shade each other's roots from the hot sun.

6. Lay out a watering system to those new plants and any established plants that are least drought resistant. Install a battery-operated timer system (available in most gardening shops). Set at a low setting. Water from March to September. Plants survive when they develop deep roots. Plants with shallow roots will not survive a long, hot summer.

7. Avoid a lawn. It will be expensive to water

FLOWERING TIMES (* = best times)

Typical plants	Feb/Mar	Apr/May	June	July/Aug	Sept	Oct/Nov	Dec/Jan
Geraniums	■	■*	■*	■	■	■	■
Gazanias	■	■*	■*			■	
Margaritas	■	■*	■			■*	
Mesembryanthemums	■	■*	■				
Bulbs (depends on type)	■*	■*	■*				■
Thyme		■	■*	■			
Rosemary	■	■*	■				
Rock roses	■	■*					
Lavender (depends on type)	■	■	■*	■*			
Aloes/Succulents		■	■				■
Roses		■*	■*	■	■	■	
Jasmine		■					
Plumbago		■	■*	■*	■		
Wisteria	■*						
Bougainvillea (can vary a lot)		■*	■*	■*	■	■*	
Bignonia		*	■*	■*	■		
Honeysuckle		■	■*				
Hibiscus		■	■*	■	■		
Lantana		■	■*	■*	■	■*	
Oleander		■	■*	■*	■		
Bottlebrush		■*					
Jacaranda		■	■				
Mimosas (depends on type)	■*	■					
Almond	■*						
Orange (fruit)	■					■	■
(flowers)	■*	■*					
Lemon (flowers and fruit)	■	■	■	■	■	■	■

The initial challenge

Starting to look after itself

and need a gardener to cut it. If used in the summer it will wear quickly in the summer sun.

8. Instead maximise the number and size of terraces and pathways. Remember that a Spanish garden is to be lived in. The house is a retreat for the occasional cold or rainy day and to sleep. Paths and terraces also provide welcome shade and moisture for the roots of plants planted nearby.

9. Spanish gardens have plenty of space for sunbathing. What is often absent is sufficient shade for summer eating, reading and siestas. So plant some drought resistant trees for shade. Possibilities include carobs, jacarandas, olives, mimosas, almonds and palms.

10. Before finalising the initial garden design and plantings look at what plants and trees survive well on nearby neglected gardens and alongside motorways. Many are very colourful, often self-seeded and don't even need the care of an absentee gardener!

11. Visit by visit progress the garden. Within a few years the garden will be luxuriant and ready for your visits or perhaps eventual full residency. Many people started as absentee gardeners, as one of us did. Eventually succeeding but learning the hard way at times.

12. Just stick with it. Don't despair if plants die. And enjoy Spain as well as gardening while you are here.

10. *Design for elderly, disabled and infirm*

Many home owners need to consider making their gardens more practical for the elderly, disabled or infirm persons. Groups of persons who have time to really enjoy a colourful and perfumed garden. But would like to do it safely on foot or in a wheelchair with or without a carer.

The following 21 guidelines are suggested when designing or modifying your garden.

1. Repair cracked and uneven paths.
2. Pave paths with non-slip surfaces.
3. Make paths wide enough for wheelchairs or two persons walking together.
4. If you have more than one level in the garden join them by gentle slopes or shallow steps.
5. Fix strong handrails alongside steps and slopes and around some of the most aromatic and colourful beds.
6. Consider constructing a number of raised beds so that leaves and flowers can be touched easily by those who cannot bend over or have impaired eyesight.
7. Ensure that ponds are surrounded by strong, secure fences with good handrails.
8. Do not plant and remove any prickly plants/shrubs such as yuccas, cacti and palms with low fronds.
9. Do not plant prickly bushes within falling distance of pathways.
10. Ensure that all hoses are constantly coiled and again away from the pathways.
11. Install a number of strategically placed seats. Ensure that they are heavy and stable. Place them so that close and more distant vistas are the best in the garden.
12. Place a firm table at reading and work height in front of one or more seats.
13. Ensure that any plant pots and urns are off the paths and not placed near the seating areas where they could trip people.
14. Give the elderly, handicapped and infirm person a bell to ring should they get into a difficult situation and need help
15. Sweep up fallen leaves daily. Even if not wet after rain they can be slippery to unsure persons.
16. Ensure that any electric switches for garden lights are safe and that the garden electric circuit has a trip separate from the main house fuse box.
17. Don't leave any unused garden tools around the garden. Put them back in a secure place immediately after use.
18. Cut back any branches that hang over paths or terraces that could catch persons or their clothing.
19. Ensure that children's toys, large and small, are not left around paths and terraces.
20. Check the strength of canvas/plastic seated garden chairs frequently and replace as soon as they show signs of wear.
21. Widen doorways of sheds and greenhouses to accommodate Zimmer frames or wheelchairs.

11. *The flower garden in January/February*

January is the best time for the major winter clean up, one of the most important and major activities in the gardening calendar.

You will have done a light autumn clean up already in October or early November. Hopefully you allowed shrubs in flower to continue doing so until Christmas. After the October rains, gardens took off following the constraints of the long dry summer. Many gardens had plenty of colour at Christmas. Often impressing visitors who had left bare bleak gardens in Northern Europe. However the growth will now be slowing down and some shrubs will be caught by early frosts in inland valleys. By January/February many plants will again be leggy or looking tired. Now is the time to do your major annual clean up. The equivalent of the autumn clean up in Northern Europe.

At this time your cutting back should be designed to encourage shape, good strong growth and the maximum of flowers during the next spring and summer. If you don't, many plants will become straggly, unshapely and won't flower at their best. This is particularly true of plants such as bougainvilleas, bignonias, galan de noche, lantanas, jasmine, honeysuckle and passionflower and of course roses. We give guidelines below for cutting back these and other plants. Naturally use your own judgement of exactly which plants to cut back and when in your garden and specific microclimate. You might cut back the second week of January in high inland areas but in the third week of February on south facing coastal slopes. Some plants like poinsettia and some bougainvilleas will still be flowering well. If so, leave for a few weeks but do complete the winter cut back by early March.

We have listed some of the commonest and easy plants. There are many more. In general everything needs to be pruned or tidied up in one way or another. One of the main problems with the winter clean up is what to do with the rubbish.

1. A shredder is a good idea especially if you have a compost heap. If you use one it is best to shred straight away while the wood is fresh. If you let rubbish dry it is much more difficult to shred.
2. Cut the rubbish up into reasonable sizes and bring to garden rubbish bins, in bags if possible.
3. Take to local dump if you have one.
4. As a last resort have a bonfire. Remember in most areas you will need to check with the town hall if you need a permit. Only burn early in the morning and preferably with no wind. Keep it small and have a hose handy. We discuss this more fully in Chapter 84.

---

1. Bougainvillea - cut back the side shoots along each of the main branches to stimulate flowering shoots. Cut back the main branches to give shape. The purple variety especially benefits from a thorough pruning. Make sure you cut out all the suckers. These are the greenish straight stems with larger leaves.

2. Lantanas - are one of the best plants in a Spanish garden. Well pruned they give colour during most months of the year. The several varieties need a slightly different treatment. Purple low growing - cut back leggy branches to half their length and trim to shape. Slow growing yellow variety - prune lightly to shape. Yellow/orange, pink/white varieties grow as shrubs - cut back hard. Cut back all flowering stems to five to 10 cm from the main trunk. The plant will look very bare but you will stimulate the sprouting of a multitude of new flowering shoots. If you are training the above colours into a standard or climbing format, cut back to shape and encourage side shoots.

3. Hibiscus - some Spanish gardeners cut these back very hard, but we don't find this necessary. A shortening of the branches by 30 to 50 cm, depending on the size of the plant will give a good shape.

4. Plumbago - shorten branches to half their length and generally tidy up. This will produce a well-shaped bush.

5. Jasmine - as plumbago.

6. Oleander - can grow very big and get quite leggy. Every second or third year it is a good idea to prune back very hard shortening all branches by a few feet so that they will branch out again. In between just keep them tidy and cut out any suckers. (Be careful when pruning oleander, the sap and flowers are poisonous).

7. Bignonia - grows rampant and must be pruned right back leaving whatever lateral woody branches you want for next year's growth.

8. Galan de Noche - should be finished flowering by now, so cut back hard.

9. Palms - cut out some lower fronds (mind the spikes), generally tidy up.

10. In the flowerbed trim back herbs (e.g. lavender, rosemary) to shape. Ensure you trim off dead flower heads. Cut back margaritas etc., to encourage spring growth. The dead leaves should be removed around gazanias; if you have large plants divide and replant where you have gaps. A few will always die in the heat of the summer. Only pull plants out if completely dead - if there is some life left you will be surprised how they recover the next spring.

11. Hedges of all types benefit from a short back and sides in the winter. Cut back the top to a height that gives you privacy without being impossible to prune safely. Trim both sides to tidy and reduce the overhang over adjacent shrubs and flowerbeds. A good trim also stimulates flowering shoots on flowering hedges. If the hedge is getting leggy cut out some of the hard, thick internal branches to stimulate new, thicker growth. We will discuss hedges in more detail in Chapter 38.

12. Roses will normally have stopped flowering by now. Cut back shrubs to two or three buds of the previous year's growth. Cut out any suckers coming up from the base. With climbers and ramblers, cut out old and week stems with few flowering shoots. Cutback the rest to shape. We will discuss roses more fully in Chapters 31, 32 and 33.

13. Keep strong cuttings from shrubs and roses and use them to propagate new plants. For some the timing will not be ideal but cuttings are free. Place them in dark wine or beer bottles in a semi-shaded position or pot up to five or six to a 15cm pot.

12. *The flower garden in March/April*

There are three main tasks for March and April. Firstly to carry out a spring clean after the major winter cut back. Secondly to plant new plants and thirdly the care of spring flowering plants.

1. A SPRING CLEAN

1. You have probably now completed the major cut back, pruning, plant splitting and clearing. Now is the time to rake up any twigs and leaves and add them to the compost heap.
2. Turn over the compost heap, adding some new material such as herb cuttings, early grass cuttings or leaves. This will prevent the compost heap from getting too wet and provide new food for resident worms. If the heap is too dry, dampen the layers.
3. Empty the tool shed or corner of the garage. Sweep and wash out. Add additional hooks, supports, separators and shelves.
4. Before putting the tools back, clean them up and lightly oil wooden handles. Oil the mechanisms of secateurs, tree pruners, saw blades etc.
5. Replace any broken or weak tool handles.
6. Sharpen shears and the cutting edge of spades and hoes etc.
7. Sort through the seed boxes and stack in planting sequence. Make a list of additional seeds required for potting up in March/April or planting out during April, May and June.
8. Clean out the garden frame. Remove any wintering snails, slugs and snakes. Spray the sides and soil with a fungicide inside and out. Horsetail is our effective natural fungicide. To prepare, pour boiling water on the dried herbs, leave 10 minutes, strain, dilute slightly and spray.
9. Wash all plastic and earthenware flowerpots in a strong washing up liquid. Rinse and stack, ready for use by size.
10. Clear out the greenhouse. Wash the windows inside and out. Then spray the inside with a fungicide.
11. Wash down the potting table and spray with a fungicide. Repaint with wood preservative.
12. Wash, check and coil garden hoses. Purchase replacement new hoses and connections.
13. Clean and oil the shredder and lawn mower. Have the blades sharpened if blunt. If they started to have problems during last year arrange for a service.
14. Sort through, wash and restack garden canes and row-marking sticks. Throw away or burn any that are weak or rotting.
15. Check through bottles and packets of garden sprays and chemicals. Make a buying list to stock up before you next need them.
16. Check and clean garden ladders, especially any with wooden parts. These can easily become weakened by internal boring insects.
17. Clean up the wheelbarrow, repaint, inflate the tyre and replace if it soon deflates.
18. Check tree support posts and ties. Knock posts in further if loose. Replace if they are starting to rot. Loosen tight ties. Make new non-rubbing ties by running wire through a short length of irrigation tube or hosepipe.
19. Check fence posts. Repair or replace. Ensure that the weight of climbing shrubs is not becoming top heavy.
20. Check that the heads are secure on rakes, scythes, hoes, trenching tools and brooms.

Completing the above tasks now will make spring and summer gardening more enjoyable and less harassing.

2. SPRING PLANTINGS

March is almost as good as October/November for planting all new perennials, shrubs and trees including those that can be affected by January and February frosts. But don't leave it too late, as newly planted plants will dry out too quickly as the weather gets hotter. This applies particularly to your young plants propagated from cuttings last Autumn.

Plant the beds to the maximum. Tall plants at the back, medium in the middle and short at the front. Choose climbers, shrubs and annuals that produce a profusion of flowers over extended periods. Plant so that all soil is covered with thick foliage or ground cover. The total shade will help retain water and suppress weeds.

Water all plants well when planted and weekly thereafter unless they show signs of wilting earlier. Don't over water. It is essential that plants start to develop deep root systems searching for water as early as possible. Feed new plants when planted with a liquid feed made up with well-rotted compost or manure and leaves of comfrey and nettle plants, or a proprietary feed. Repeat monthly. More detailed instructions for planting are included in Chapter 27. A wide choice of plants are discussed in later chapters.

- Summer annuals can now be planted out progressively. They are discussed in detail in Chapter 27. Annuals need regular watering and feeding. We use the same feed as mentioned above for shrubs etc.
- If you find packets of summer bulbs in garden centres or even in your garage it is not too late to plant them.
- As the weather warms up try raising some exotic perennials from seed, especially if you have a garden frame or greenhouse.

3. CARE OF EXISTING PLANTS

a. Dead head, dead head and dead head to stimulate long flowering periods for spring perennials and annuals.
b. Keep an eye open for the geranium moth. Read Chapter 19 for solutions.
c. As the weather warms up increase your watering.
d. Feed plants monthly.
e. Tie in climbers such as sweet peas and passion flowers.
f. Check for signs of mealy bugs. Found mainly on pot plants. Remove and squash. Spray with neem - a non-toxic insecticide - to reduce the possibility of further infestations.
g. If you have water lilies that lacked vigour last year now is a good time to put special fertiliser blocks into their pots.
h. If not done in the January clean up remove any low and drooping palm fronds which could be dangerous to passers by.
i. Check that you have removed all pointed ends of yuccas and cacti. They can be painful! The more work done in the garden now the better the spring and summer garden.

13. *The flower garden in May/June*

May and June are an important time in the flower garden. Essential tasks include planting out, watering, mulching, feeding, dead heading, plant protection, tying up, topping up the compost heap and raising some exotic flowers from seed.

1. PLANTING OUT

This is the main time for planting out annuals to give good summer displays in the flowerbeds and terrace pots.
The easiest plants are:
- petunias, busy lizzies and fuchsias
- gazanias, geraniums, portulacas.

2. WATERING

- Watering will need to be increased as the weather heats up. Especially if we have no spring storms.
- Turn up the frequency of watering systems and check that all nozzles flow freely.
- Ensure that annuals planted during March or April are not allowed to dry out slowing their growth and bud development.
- Ensure that any newly planted annuals and perennial plants are watered every day or every second day, depending on the temperatures and the exposure of your garden to drying winds.

3. MULCHING

- Ensure that any shrubs planted out during March and April are well mulched.
- Mulch around sweet peas with well-rotted compost.
- Mulch heavily any hedges or trees planted since last autumn. Preferably with well-rotted compost or manure. This will help prevent the soil around the root balls from drying out as well as adding beneficial nutrients.
- Mulch around delicate small cacti and rockery plants with a centimetre of course grit or lava chippings.
- If not done earlier, clear any dead leaves and twigs from around the base of your roses and mulch well with horse manure. Our experience is that this is more effective than using a proprietary rose feed, as the manure feeds as well as protecting roots from the scorching sun. This is particularly important with any first year bushes you may have started from cuttings.

4. DEAD HEADING

- Deadhead plants as flowers die back to ensure that energy goes into the production of new flowers rather than seed heads. The only exception being to leave a few flowers to ripen if you plan to collect you own seed for next year. Early flowers are said to produce the most reliable and strong seeds as they develop and dry under ideal conditions.
- If you deadhead early flowering plants such as poppies and hollyhocks you can extend their flowering season considerably.
- Cut back roses to a new outward facing bud.
- Pick bunches of sweet peas for the house. This will stimulate a longer flowering period.

5. PLANT PROTECTION

- Watch out for emergent black fly, whitefly, moth, butterfly and caterpillar damage... and of course any invasion of slugs or snails.
- Spray against blackfly and whitefly with a dilute solution of potassium soap or neem, a natural extract from a south east Asian tree.
- Spray against moths, butterflies and caterpillars with garlic sprays.
- Preferably use snail traps, or other ecological methods to reduce/prevent slug damage. As a last resort use slug pellets.
- We will look at plant protection in more detail in Chapter 55.

6. TYING UP

- Tie up climbing plants such as honeysuckle, sweet peas and passionflowers as they grow.
- Tie in climbing and rambling roses to a pergola or frame. Likewise with tall bougainvilleas.

7. TOPPING UP THE COMPOST HEAP

- Ensure that any soft cuttings, flower heads and kitchen vegetable waste is added to compost heap.
- Keep the composting material moist and accelerate with fresh manure or an accelerator.

8. RAISING EXOTIC PLANTS FROM SEED

The temperatures in May/June are ideal for germinating seeds from other Mediterranean areas or sub-tropical areas.
Now is a good time to raise some exotic plants from seed. Ambient temperatures will be at the level required for good germination with no need for an electrically heated propagator or heated greenhouse.

The advantages of growing from seed are several.
1. If successful your annuals and perennials are less expensive than plants purchased in the nursery.
2. You can attempt to raise unusual plants from different parts of the world that have a Mediterranean or sub-tropical climate. The best catalogue we know for searching out the unexpected is Chiltern Seeds Tel 00 44 1229 581137 - email: info@chilternseeds.co.uk. We have recently planted exotic passionflowers and alstroemeria from South Africa and a blue water lily from South Africa.
3. You can raise the plants in the climate in which they will be planted. There will be less shock than with plants that move between growers and garden centres often in two different countries.
4. You can swap spares with gardening friends or give as unusual presents.

Unfortunately, many people are unsuccessful with seeds, including us at times. There are many reasons. At this stage we offer the following basic guidelines.

1. Follow the planting and germination instructions on the packet or in the catalogue to the letter. It is important to recognise that we are trying to raise plants from seeds in a much hotter climate than we were used to before we came to Spain.

2. Plant seeds individually or in pairs in damp compost in the segments of preformed plastic trays. In this way you can cut out and move on the earliest seedlings before they become leggy.

3. Place the plastic trays inside polystyrene fish boxes. Look for them outside the local supermarket. A wash removes any fish smell! These trays retain water and heat better than wooden seed boxes or plant pots. Make a few holes in the base to allow drainage.

4. Water the planted trays with water to which a few drops of a natural fungicide has been added.

5. Enclose the planted box in a sheet of clear plastic. Roll over the plastic to create a seal and hold closed with clothes pegs.

6. Place the sealed boxes in a warm, semi-shaded part of the garden or in a shaded garden frame or greenhouse.

7. Watch for emerging seedlings. When they are two cm high cut out the appropriate tray segments and move them into individual sealed plastic bags.

8. When four cm high, open up the bags, harden off plantlets and grow on, never allowing the plantlets to dry out.

9. When strong plants have formed, plant out or pot on into larger pots.

We hope the above guidelines improve your success rate.

14. *The flower garden in July/August*

We are now entering the hottest weeks of the year. No doubt you want to reduce physical work and the time spent on it to a minimum. However there are many useful jobs that need doing in the flower garden. We suggest the following as the essential jobs. They are best done in the early morning, during the evening or on the occasional cooler day.

1. The removal of the dead flower heads of flowering plants and shrubs, such as geraniums, petunias, margaritas and oleanders, will stimulate new flower buds and reduce the plant energy spent on producing seeds.

2. Dead head the bottlebrush to stimulate extra side shoots and therefore more flowers next year.

3. If you wish to gather some ripe seeds for sowing in the autumn or the following spring, leave selected large seed heads on the plants to ripen. Pick when fully dry and dry further for two weeks in a dry place in full sun. Then store in airtight plastic containers until planting time. (Don't forget to label them). Avoid glass containers, as these are dangerous if dropped and broken in the garage or garden.

4. Prune back plants that flower on long stems and spikes when they have finished flowering. These include, roses, lavender, echium and rosemary. The latter can be dried in the sun for cooking or for a stimulating breakfast infusion.

5. Prune unsightly branches on lantanas, bougainvilleas and plumbago. Also remove dead flower heads that are turning to seed heads. Both will generate new flowering shoots.

6. Dead head bulbous plants that have flowered but leave the stems to dry back to strengthen the bulbs and corms. Such plants include lilies, cannas and gladioli.

7. Dead head geraniums and remove any damaged or dry shoots. Watch for the geranium moth. Spray regularly with a proprietary insecticide or use a natural spray made up from an infusion of garlic, or try putting a drop of essential oil of rosemary in water.

8. Streptosolens will now be in full flower. Deadhead and keep damp to stimulate continuous flowering. Although the plants look similar to lantanas they need more care and attention. In particular they are not as drought or cold resistant and are susceptible to mildew in humid conditions.

9. Ensure that ponds are topped up regularly. Have fountains on as many hours as possible to keep the water aerated. Cut off dead flower heads and stalks from water lilies. This will stimulate follow on flowering and reduce the accumulation of rubbish in the pond.

10. If very hot in August watch out for the drying out and falling of leaves on fruit trees, especially apricots, peaches and cherries. Give them a good soak if this occurs, otherwise some branches may die back.

11. Check for fungal infections on plants like fuchsia and mandevilla etc., and spray with dilute horsetail or any other ecological fungicide.

12. If you have a lawn, raise the mower blade an inch and reduce the frequency of cutting. Leave the cuttings on the lawn to mulch the roots. This will stimulate a healthy lawn. It will also reduce the amount of water needed to keep the lawn alive.

13. Sweep up fallen leaves and put them on the compost heap. Collect carob pods as they fall and store in a dry place. These can be bagged up and sold for cash at the end of August/ early September.

14. Water annuals daily and any other plants recently planted - climbers, plants in pots and garden beds - that will continue to flower. Don't waste water on plants that are normally dormant after flowering. They will soon recover from the drought in the autumn.

15. Check the watering system for leaks and clean out any blocked spray heads. Adjust the timer system to operate at night but at a low volume to preserve scarce water. Recognise any local controls and bans that may exist in your area.

16. Give flowering plants in pots a good feed of dilute comfrey and liquid manure, or any other proprietary liquid feed to stimulate ongoing flowering.

17. If you have a grapevine, give a light dusting of sulphur in July - to protect the ripening fruit from fungi (use sparingly by putting sulphur in a sock and shaking over the plant in the early morning or late evening).

18. Cut and hang up ripened sunflowers to dry for eating or for winter bird food.

19. Ensure that you use your summer garden to the full.

20. Don't let gardening chores take up too much of your time. The cooler autumn will be a better time for major initiatives.

15. *The flower garden in September/October*

As the weather starts to cool during September and the days shorten, gardens are coming back to life again. With some autumn rains, we can look forward to colourful gardens during October and November, when lantanas, margaritas, bougainvilleas etc., can again be in full bloom. Even light pruning has been risky during the hottest summer weeks - a sure way of killing off many plants that dry out. But now is the time to do a tidy-up but not the major winter clean out. That's for later.

The following are among the most important jobs.

1. Rake or pick up dead leaves and put them on the compost heap. Continue weekly until the deciduous flowering and fruit trees have lost all their leaves.

2. Rake up and store any fallen almonds and walnuts missed when picked last month. Also collect and sell the last of the carob pods.

3. Trim back herb plants. Cut back to shape, removing dead flowers and unshapely long shoots. Rosemary and lavender can be cut back hard, especially if you are training them into low hedges in the garden.

4. Most hedges need a tidy up. Wait for the sap to stop rising before doing a major hedge shearing in December or January.

5. Plumbagos are probably still flowering so merely cut back flowered shoots and overgrowing branches.

6. Many bougainvilleas are still flowering and others starting to bud up for an autumn display, so only cut out dead shoots, straggly branches and suckers or watershoots. The latter are easy to recognise. They have paler green stems and bigger leaves and normally grow straight up.

7. If your geraniums have been attacked by the African butterfly, cut them back hard below any damage. If very bad, take the plant out and burn. On healthy plants continue to dehead and remove dead leaves several times a week. To stimulate autumn flowering give them a good feed.

8. Lantanas may have become leggy with shoots covered in ripening berries. Cut out long branches and trim back the shoots with berries. Lantanas can be stimulated to flower until January. Their colourful Christmas display is invaluable. Hisbiscus and other flowering shrubs also benefit from a light pruning to develop their shape and stimulate further flowering shoots.

9. Healthy annuals will have survived the hot summer. A good clean up and feed will encourage a few more weeks of flowers.

10. New growth is appearing on many shrubs and succulents. It is therefore a good time to take cuttings of the various plants you are pruning. Pot up 20/25cm cuttings and keep them in a shady place. Keep moist.

11. When tidying up, now is a good time to take seeds of lantanas, marigolds and margaritas. Also of San Pedro, the metre-high white, yellow and pink pretty wild flowers you see growing along the roadside outside many villages. San Pedro can be sown in the spring in pots or directly into the soil. Once established, the deep-rooted plant will need little attention and will selfseed. The major attractions of San Pedro are the evening perfume and the profusion of mixed colour patterns and hues that develop after a few years by cross-pollination.

12. It is important to remember that plants in Spain behave differently to Northern Europe. In Northern Europe flowering will be at an end in September and September/October is the time for a major garden clean up. On the Mediterranean coast, resist this. If you are a gardener, ignore the demands of departing or absentee owners. A major cut back now will destroy the colourful Christmas garden.

16. *The flower garden in November/December*

November and December are important months in our gardens. Now is the time to start redesigns and new plantings. The main jobs during these two colder months are:

- autumn plantings of perennials, shrubs and trees.
- light pruning of perennials and shrubs continuing to flower.
- the planting of winter annuals to brighten the garden for Christmas.

We look at each in turn.

1. AUTUMN PLANTING OF PERENNIALS, SHRUBS AND TREES

The second half of October and November are good times to make many new plantings in our hot climate. We say this for a number of reasons.

a. The soil is easier to dig and less watering will be required to establish new plants. Provided of course that you have had some autumn rain, if not a full 'gota fria'.
b. The days are now cool enough for heavy work in the garden.
c. New plants will dry out slower with the shorter and cooler days.
d. Plants will have six months to establish good root systems before the hot weather of next May and June.
e. With luck the compost heap established in the spring is ready to dig into the soil when planting.
f. There are unlikely to be water restrictions to prevent the regular watering of new plantings.
g. Garden centres are generally well stocked.
h. We have had time to reflect on the successes and failures of our gardens during the last spring and summer. Now is the time to decide what we would like to add or change ready for next year, as well as to brighten up the winter garden.

On the coastal plain most things can be planted, as there is little chance of frost. However if you live in an inland valley, especially on the north facing slopes, hold back on the planting of semi hardy shrubs such as bougainvillea, hibiscus etc., until the spring. To ensure you spend money wisely first prepare a list of the gaps you want to fill and the changes you want to make in the garden layout, mix of colours and heights. Then list the plants you wish to purchase or visit a few garden centres looking for ideas.

When you buy be sure to buy strong well-shaped plants. Look at the bottom of the pot to check that roots are starting to come through the holes. There is nothing worse than buying plants that are merely recently planted cuttings. November is an excellent time for planting roses whether purchased as potted plants, bare root or raised from cuttings. The choices available are enormous.

Planting

If you have poor soil dig a hole two or three times as deep as the existing root system of the plant to be planted. With good soil one and half times as deep should suffice. Then fill the hole with water and let the water soak away. Half fill the hole with well-rotted compost or manure and mix well - tread down well then half fill again with a compost soil mix. Put the plant in the hole spreading any visible roots. Make firm and then top up firming the soil layer by layer. Leave the top of the soil two centimetres below the surrounding soil to aid watering until established. Water well and then when the top surface starts to dry out water again. Keep new plants moist but not under swamp conditions. Feed in the spring with an appropriate proprietary fertilizer or a liquid made up from well-rotted manure, comfrey leaves and nettle leaves. If you buy bare rooted shrubs or trees make sure that they are soaked in a bucket of water for 24 hours before planting.

2. LIGHT PRUNINGS

Cut back dead flower heads and untidy shoots on perennials and shrubs, especially lantanas, bougainvilleas and jasmine. Each can give wonderful displays until January. Remember major pruning is done in January.

3. PLANTING WINTER ANNUALS

The main planting for beds and pots will be late petunias and pansies.

4. OTHER JOBS

- If you haven't planted spring bulbs yet it is not too late. Bulbs in pots can be forced in a dark room or cellar.
- Generally keep paths, terraces and flowerbeds tidy. If you do weedkill, now is a good time to spray the drive.
- Now is also a good time to start to construct rockeries, ponds, garden frames and a greenhouse. Also to build new paths and terraces.
- Check your autumn cuttings to ensure that they are starting well and not drying out.
- Bring dormant potted poinsettias and Christmas cacti in from their hiding places in the garden. Tidy up, water more regularly and feed. Ours normally flower at Christmas but we have recently been told that they would be even better if we treated them as follows: Mid-November start to put plants in a dark cupboard from 17.00 to 09.00 daily. During the day bring them out into a bright terrace. When they start to come into flower keep them out all the time.
- If you have several single newly rooted cuttings of Christmas cacti transplant them into one large pot. This will develop into a mass of flowers. Hopefully they will be even better if you treat as above!
- Water lilies will have died back. Remove dead leaves and stems. Take out the largest plants. Trim and split. Repot into weighted pots. If you now have too many for your pond pass on the spares to friends.
- Water lunar lemon tree to fatten lemons for Christmas. Also other citrus trees if the autumn has been dry.
- Check plants such as fuchsia and roses for disease. If they are infested with mealy bug, wipe off with damp cloth and spray with neem, an ecological insecticide or any other proprietary insecticide.
- If not done already turn off the garden watering system.

17. Propagation

Propagation from cuttings is an important autumn task. October is the best month.

ADVANTAGES OF PROPAGATION

The advantages of propagation are:

1. The production of new plants from old at little expense, provided care is taken.
2. There are many plants that can be reproduced from cuttings: Herbs, shrubs, perennials, including geraniums, succulents and ground cover plants and many more.
3. You know that your cuttings have been taken from healthy plants.
4. You can develop strong plants over the winter for spring planting.
5. A garden frame or greenhouse is not necessary but can be helpful.

POTTING UP CUTTINGS

1. It is very important to have a good light compost that drains well. By now you should have good friable compost from your kitchen compost heap.

2. Mix in some proprietary seed compost and some gritty sand to make it lighter.

3. If you don't have your own compost mix earth, seed compost and sand.

4. Put mix in large container. Add just enough water to dampen it evenly. For a large amount we add a capful of liquid nettle and comfrey to enrich it.

5. Select a range of different sized plastic flowerpots. Wash them ready for potting. Remember your cuttings will vary in size, e.g. small lavender shoots to woody hibiscus.

6. Put gravel or small pieces of broken pots at base for drainage.

7. Fill with compost mix and firm down.

8. Put cuttings into prepared pots. Depending on size you can put three or four to each pot. We prefer one in each, as they won't need to be divided later and potted on. At the time of planting out, a good tip is to cut the side and base of the pot so that plants can be removed undamaged.

9. Put each pot in a clear plastic bag. Prop up bag with a length of old 'drip feed' black tubing so that the leaves don't touch the plastic. Especially in the case of grey leaved plants. Close the bag.

10. An alternative to the above is to use polystyrene fish boxes - most supermarkets throw them out. Wash well and make holes in the base for drainage. Cover with a damp layer of compost/soil mix about three centimetres deep. Fill with planted pots. Or fill completely with potting compost and plant lots of small cuttings. Or alternatively plant the latter in small plastic planting trays and sit them in the fish box with just the fine layer of soil beneath. It will make it easier for re-potting later. Whatever you do cover the boxes completely with white plastic - you can buy it by the metre from garden shops. Allow it to overlap and close with clothes pegs for easy opening.

11. Both the above will form a good microclimate, if sealed properly, for the cuttings and you won't need to worry about watering until they are ready to harden off apart from checking them from time to time. Before you close them up spray with an infusion of horsetail or an ecological fungicide.

12. If you don't use the 'microclimate' method prepare as in 1-8. Then line plastic trays or similar with three centimetres of compost/soil mix. Stand pots on soil. Put in semi shady place or garden frame that is protected from the hot sun. If you keep the soil underneath moist, the plants shouldn't dry out.

13. Remember to label your cuttings. For inexpensive labels - find some old plastic blinds. Remove vanes. Cut into strips and mark with a waterproof pen.

PREPARING CUTTINGS

On soft wooded plants such as lavender, rosemary, sage, plumbago, fuchsias, geraniums etc., pull off a side shoot together with heel. It is preferable to have a leaf node at the tip and base of the cutting. Pinch out growing tip. Remove any flowers or buds. Leave at most four leaves. Shorten if necessary. Smaller cuttings grow stronger.

a. Geraniums and succulents like to be left to dry for a few days before potting up.

b. On woody shrubs such as lantana, bougainvilleas and hibiscus cut off a side branch and cut into 10 to 15cm lengths with a bud at the base and top. Obviously you can also use prunings trimmed in the same way.

c. Lantana can be propagated as softwood or hardwood and also grown from seed.

ONGOING CARE AND HARDENING OFF

1. Examine regularly. If the cuttings look healthy leave alone. If they have rotted throw the whole pot in the bin. Be careful, don't act too hastily. They can appear dormant one day and start sprouting the next!

2. Potting On. Once groups of the smaller cuttings have rooted well, pot on into slightly bigger pots. And look after as in point number 12 (potting up cuttings). Some of the larger plants may benefit from being potted on. But generally most cuttings, once established and hardened off, can be planted direct into their final position.

3. Harden off. Once cuttings in pots appear to be growing well remove plastic. Keep in a semi-shaded place and make sure they don't dry out.

4. Planting out. When roots start to show at the base of the pot. Plant into final position in early spring. Nurse carefully until they really take root. Make sure they don't dry out.

FEEDING

Once the cuttings have produced leaves feed with a dilute solution of liquid comfrey and nettle or a proprietary plant food once a week.

The taking of cuttings year after year is an interesting and inexpensive way of filling up the garden. But take plenty of cuttings - they are free. If you achieve a 70 per cent success rate you will be doing well. Extra plants can always be swapped with friends.

18. *Gazanias*

Gazanias are one of the most useful low growing bedding plants in Mediterranean gardens. They are grown for both the brilliance of their flowers and the attractiveness of the green or silver ground covering leaves.

The flowers are large and daisy like. They come in a wide range of single and multi-hued colours - cream, yellow, orange, burnt red and purple. Cared for they produce a continuous flowering through the spring, early summer and autumn. In the hottest weeks of July and August and the winter they are normally dormant.

Gazanias thrive in a sunny position but they can also do well in semi-shaded positions. There are three popular formats of gazanias. A low growing variety generally with yellow or orange flowers and silver leaves. This is excellent for ground cover. Grow as a carpet at the front of a perennial bed or as clumps in the rockery.

The multi-hued varieties are taller and clump forming and generally have green leaves. These are excellent for planting in groups between other perennials. A more leggy variety is also available. This looks dramatic cascading over a terrace. The other varieties need no pruning. However, deheading and watering in dry spells encourage continuous flowering. Just watch how gazanias respond to a heavy summer storm. When water is scarce or cut off, established gazanias survive as they are very drought resistant. They need little feeding except in poorer soils. Then a spring feed can be particularly beneficial.

Propagation is easy and an inexpensive way to increase the number of gazanias in the garden. Rooted cuttings can be pulled from the side of the low spreading varieties. These can be planted directly into the garden. When the clump forming varieties have matured they can be easily dug up and divided into several plants. These can also be planted directly in the garden or potted up for a few months. But remember to water them!

Side shoots can also be pulled off the clump varieties but they will need to be potted up for a few months until a good root ball has grown. Cuttings and new plants are best planted between March and May or in October/November. Like most plants they do need regular watering for the first few months after planting. Once established watering can be cut back.

19. Geraniums

Existing plants

One of the highlights of gardens on the Costa used to be the profusion of healthy geraniums - multicoloured, long-flowering geraniums in pots, in beds and tumbling down terrace walls. Sadly, such sights have been on the decline in recent years The cause is the unfortunate importation of the African geranium moth. This first came to Mallorca in the 80s and then spread to the mainland in the 90s. The original source of the moth is thought to have been South Africa. This insignificant small brown moth has, like a plague, reduced the geranium, or more correctly named "pelargonium", to a rarity or short-lived plant in many gardens and villages.

However, there are indications that geraniums are making a comeback. Surviving old plants seem to have developed some resistance so that cuttings can be planted successfully. Healthy new plants are increasingly available and can survive with care. But first clean up your existing plants. Cut off all stems with holes and dark patches. Please burn or put in bin. Do not put on the compost heap. On the plus side, the base of a totally cut-back plant may well sprout and produce an excellent plant.

New plants

Buy only healthy strong growing plants. Preferably with many buds but few flowers open unless you want an instant impact. Be alert for any signs of geranium moth damage. If you see moths fluttering over the plants beware. It may be best to move onto another garden centre. And most importantly purchase the most appropriate type of geraniums for your garden beds and pots.

There are three popular types of geraniums (pelargoniums).

First the *pelargonium regals*. These generally have multicoloured flowers and fancy crinkly heart shaped leaf. These are best grown in flower beds rather than pots.

Secondly, the more common *zonal geraniums* with rounded leaves in a variety of colours. A wide range of flower colours is available with single, semi double or double petals. In most gardens these do best grown in pots on balconies or terraces. But one does still see large shrub like specimens in gardens that have survived the geranium moth.

Thirdly there are the trailing varieties, the *ivy leaf geraniums* sometimes known as 'Murcianas'. Again you will find single and double flowers in a wide range of single or multiple colours. An interesting plant collection can be built up by purchase and from neighbours' cuttings.

These geraniums have many uses in the garden. They look well in window boxes and pots as well as tumbling down banks and terraces. Geraniums are survivors. They survive big changes of temperature and the hardship of having absentee gardeners. But to achieve a long flowering season they do need care.

Ensure that geraniums are potted in a well drained soil. In hot weather pots need to be watered every second day. But they will survive a total drying out. Fed once a week geraniums may well flower all the year round.

In the garden geraniums will grow in most soils, but they need a watering and feeding twice a week until established. To keep plants healthy keep them clean. Remove dead flowers and leaves weekly and be on the constant alert for the damage caused by the African geranium moth boring and laying eggs in the fleshy stems (look out for black patches). In the spring and summer spray twice a week with a proprietary insecticide. You can also try a simple organic spray made from crushed garlic and water. We used it. The moths certainly didn't like it and all our plants survived.

Also watch out for rust attacks on leaves. Remove and burn the leaves.

One last thought. We have found that geraniums like to be root bound. Do not pot on into bigger pots too early. Also try leaving new plants in their plastic pots. Just cut out the base before planting the whole pot in good soil in a large garden pot.

Pelargoniums in flower

20. *Lantanas*

Lantanas are an excellent shrub for Costa gardens. They flower most months, thrive in poor soils, sun and high temperatures and are also very hardy, resisting heavy frosts in the hills.

The abundance of bright coloured flat flowers are also a major attraction for butterflies. Lantanas come in a number of colours with a variety of heights and spreads. These are summarised below.

Colour	Typical height	Typical spread
Mauve/white	25cm	50cm
Yellow	75cm	1 metre
White	1 metre	1.5 metres
Pink	1 metre	1.5 metres
Orange/red	1.5 metres	2 metres

The latter is often referred to as 'Lantana Bandera' as the colours match the colours of the Spanish flag. As well as the normal shrub the Bandera can also be grown as a standard or climber. Lantanas can be planted between other plants or shrubs in a mixed bed. However for maximum effect they are best planted in groups. A bed of mixed colours and varying heights can look spectacular.

The low growing mauve and white varieties are good for ground cover and cascading over banks.

Lantanas are not difficult to grow well provided a few basic guidelines are followed.

1. PURCHASE

Look for plants with signs of strong new growth and buds and with a good root system. Small plants soon grow so there is little point in purchasing large specimens. If you purchase them in the dormant period from January to March they will often have been heavily pruned with little new growth. This is normal. However this does not apply to the white and mauve trailing varieties, which will normally flower throughout the winter.

2. PLANTING

Plant as for any shrub. Dig a hole larger than the root ball. Line with well rotted compost, cover with some soil. Fill hole with water and allow to soak in. Plant your plant, infill with good soil, firm in well and water.

3. WATERING

Lantanas need regular watering until their roots are established. If they have been planted in good soil and are well established they need little water. Only water when the flower heads droop. But if they are in poorer soil they will need more water to grow and flower well. A drip system works well in this case. For special occasions copious watering as the flower buds appear will achieve a peak of colour. But it is not socially responsible throughout the summer. Generally lantanas can flower continuously from April through to January and must be one of the most useful plants for producing a show of colour with little effort and little water.

4. FEEDING

Profuse flowering can be stimulated by a liquid feed twice a year. But most established plants will not need it.

5. DEADHEADING

When flowers die remove any heads that form berry-like seeds to stimulate flowering and keep pathways clean.

6. PRUNING

Apart from deadheading trim to keep in shape throughout the flowering season. This will stimulate new growth and continuous flowering. In January cut back hard to two buds from the main trunk even if still in flower. A lighter winter cut back will result in straggly plants the following year. Don't worry, new shoots will appear by March. The only exceptions are the mauve and white low growing varieties, which only need trimming to shape.

7. PROPAGATION

Lantanas can be propagated from woody cuttings by pulling off new side shoots. You may find lantanas self-seeding around the garden. Blackbirds love the berries.

With care lantanas last for many years.

21. Oleanders

The oleander is an important shrub of Mediterranean origin that grows well as a specimen bush or as a hedge.

Oleanders must be one of the best flowering and easily maintained shrubs. They adapt to most soils and withstand drought conditions. Daily we see and admire them for their long pointed dark green leaves and mass of flowers. We see them in the centre of motorways, along country lanes, in public parks, in dry river beds and in most gardens in one form or another. The flowers can be single or double in a range of colours; red, pink, peach, salmon, cream and white. In general the red, pink and white flowering varieties grow the most vigorously. As well as the single colour dark green leaves there is also an attractive variegated variety with green and cream leaves.

Oleanders can be grown as a hedge in front of a wall or wire fence, as groups of three or four in island beds, as a screen around the swimming pool or dining-out terrace to provide privacy and a wind break, or even as a specimen tree and in pots.

For a hedge, plant one colour or a mix of colours 60cm apart. In good soil conditions and watering in dry spells a two-metre high hedge can be created within four or five years. Maintain shape by pruning after flowering. This will stimulate a longer flowering period. To prevent the lower levels of a hedge from becoming leggy, cut back some of the long stems annually or every second year to 30cm from the base to stimulate low growth. Do not cut back to soil level. If you inherit a tall leggy hedge, cut it back to a metre high. It will soon recover and produce a thicker hedge. Grown as individual plants within the garden they can be grown to any height. Oleanders serve a similar purpose within Spanish gardens as the rhododendron does in the more northerly cooler climates. In fact, they are often mistaken for rhododendrons by new residents and visitors.

By careful pruning and staking, a dramatic tree can be produced with a one to two metre stem much like a mature mimosa but with thicker foliage. Oleanders are also useful for planting in large pots for the terrace. In such conditions their growth will be stunted by the restricted root ball. Pruning to create a rounded plant will produce a flower covered plant as attractive in flower as an azalea.

A word of warning. Whatever form of oleander you are pruning, wear gloves! The leaves, flowers, sap of oleanders are poisonous. If you use a shredder for garden rubbish do not under any circumstances compost oleander prunings, or use them for mulching.

Oleander plants are not expensive to purchase. But look for squat rounded versus elongated plants that need immediate pruning. Make large holes for planting. Fill with water then add compost and peat substitute. Plant the root ball in the moist mush, top up with soil and firm down. Although it is possible to plant oleanders at any time of the year October/November is the best time in practice The plants then have a chance to settle down during the winter and spring before flowering the following hot summer. Although mature bushes withstand drought, water new plants frequently during the first year. A drip feed is very beneficial.

Oleanders can easily be propagated from cuttings of mature stems. One-metre cuttings can be planted in their final planned position or a nursery bed. Plant so that only 20cms are above the ground. Water so that cuttings do not dry out. Shorter 60cm cuttings can be rooted in dark red wine bottles or brown beer bottles filled with water. Keep in semi shade. A good root ball can develop in three to six months. Then plant out carefully with plenty of peat substitute or compost in the autumn. Expect about a 30 per cent success rate by this method.

Apart from the pruning discussed earlier, the only other care oleanders need is a chemical or natural insecticide spray against greenfly and black scale should it occur.

22. *Succulent terrace pots*

Succulents are important plants in Spain. They are eye catching and easy to care for... Spaniards have always used succulents in pots and beds to add interest to both main gardens and sunny inner courtyards. Many wise international residents and absentee gardeners have followed suit. Succulents are an excellent alternative to geraniums and even thirsty annuals. Planted in terracota pots they can look good on the naya, along the terrace and around the pool. Interesting features can be achieved by planting pots with either a single specimen plant or a mix of smaller plants. Interesting specimen plants are available currently in most nurseries. There are many varieties with a range of colours, leaf shape and growing habit. However, to achieve a balanced collection of tall and low growing varieties you may need to visit a number of nurseries. For a start ask for aeoniums, mesems, sedums, mesembryanthemums, livingstone daisies, lampranthus and carpobrotus and look out for unusual specimens.

Succulents are popular for a number of reasons. They look good all the year round. They are evergreen and many flower, some in the winter. A good example is the aeonium which has a spectacular yellow pyramid flower to brighten any terrace at Christmas. Most withstand the extremes of temperature and rainfall of the coastal and inland areas. They thrive in full sun and also in semi-shade. Storing water in their leaves and stems they are the camels of the garden. Once established they need little attention. Water only when the pots are really dry and feed occasionally. The only pruning required is the removal of dry leaves and occasional pruning to shape. Most importantly most prunings can be potted up to provide an expanding collection of plants for pots, the rockery and general garden beds. Before planting prunings allow the cut ends to dry out in the sun. Then pot up in a damp mix of garden soil, peat and sand. This mix will stimulate root growth and provide essential drainage. Just keep succulents damp. They can withstand drought but can also rot off under swamp conditions.

Over a number of years you should be able to build up an interesting collection of succulents by purchases or the swapping of cuttings with friends. With patience they can also be raised from seed.

Most gardeners do not have a vegetable plot. However, excellent new potatoes can be grown in less than a square metre in the corner of a terrace or garden. Yes, this is nothing to do with succulents. But a large pot or tyre pile makes an interesting feature; plus potatoes for a summer salad.

Collect four old car tyres and pick out four good sized potatoes with sprouting eyes next time you shop. Stack the four tyres to create a large pot. Fill the bottom tyre with a mixture of soil, garden compost, kitchen waste and manure if available (not fresh). Press the four potatoes into this soil and cover with the soil mix up to the level of the second tyre. Water to keep the pile damp. When the first leaves appear, cover them and repeat several times until all four tyres are full. Healthy plants will grow out of the top. After flowering you should harvest new potatoes for summer salads.

23. Spectacular flowering plants

Most of our gardens benefit from a few spectacular flowering plants; plants that have vivid colours, an unusual format, or both; plants that stand out from all others at their time of flowering.

The following selections are among our favourites. One of the most spectacular succulents is the agave attenuata. The photograph shows a plant that flowers from early March to mid May. The small creamy flowers develop and open from the bottom up week by week. Unfortunately, the enormous curving flower stem is never fully covered with flowers. But this does not detract from the impact of the plant. Just one word of warning, a flowering plant is probably four or five years old.

From mid March to early May the echiums are in flower. The dark blue is much more spectacular than the light blue. However, a dark blue plant with a background of two light blue plants can be very impressive. Cuttings can be taken during June and July. They root easily in the summer heat. But keep plantlets well watered. Plant them out in October. With luck, they will flower the following spring.

The red bottle brush is very spectacular when it flowers in May. It comes in both bush and standard formats. The flowers look like a bottle brush and are some 15cm by 4cm in size. Each year you will have more and more flowers that form at the end of each branch. Prune lightly after flowering to stimulate new flowering shoots.

A group of blue flowering agapanthus bulbs can look exotic during July. They can be planted successfully in the flowerbeds or large pots in full sun and shade. After a few years dig up the plants in the autumn and divide the clump into three, or four, smaller clumps. Year by year you can achieve a more and more spectacular patch.

For a summer, shady spot a white, orange or yellow flowering datura can look spectacular. Its large, hanging trumpet-shaped flowers look very exotic throughout July and August. Datura do not like wind and can grow to a height of two or three metres and two metres across. So, give a plant plenty of room to look its best. They are a thirsty plant and require regular watering and feeding during the summer months to keep at their best. A word of warning, the flowers and leaves are poisonous if chewed. Warn children not to collect the tempting trumpets.

For the winter, nothing can beat a large poinsettia bush up to two metres high. The bright red bracts that surround a bunch of small yellow flowers are normally at their best in November and December. Buy a fully green plant from a nursery in October rather than the hot house forced plants sold towards Christmas. The latter are prepared as houseplants and often do not survive the transplant to the garden. Plant in well-drained soil in a sheltered sunny position. When established, prune after flowering. Take care to wear plastic gloves, as the white sap is poisonous and a skin irritant.

The above are only thought starters. You will find others in the better nurseries. Or be adventurous, try growing some from seed.

24. *Climbing plants*

Climbers can add much beauty, colour and perfume to Mediterranean gardens. Most climbers are not original natives of Spain. However over the last five centuries the range of readily available showy climbers has become very extensive.

Climbers from many parts of the world flourish in our climate. They climb by clinging, intertwining or scrambling up any support. They lend themselves to many uses. For instance growing up house or garden walls, covering pergolas and trellis or climbing up through mature trees. We will look at each situation in turn.

First, what are attractive climbers for the walls of the house? High on the list must come the various colours of bougainvillea which flower for many months. Wisteria is another showy possibility but its spring flowering period is short. It is probably better grown climbing up through a mature tree or along a garden fence intertwined with a deciduous bignonia for follow on colour.

Naturally roses are another choice. They add not only valuable colour for several months but also perfumes.

Although not really a climber, a galán de noche is a wonderful plant to train up a wall near the terrace or naya. Its deep perfume is exotic on a hot summer evening. The "bandera" orange and yellow form of lantana can also be trained as a colourful climber as can the blue flowering plumbago.

The yellow spring flowering jasmine is also useful in a corner of the house wall.

Moving to garden walls the various types of bignonia can give long lasting colourful displays.

In a good soil morning glory can soon cover a fence or wall with its bright blue flowers. They can also be trained to cover a dead tree or grow to cover an ill placed telegraph pole. The same is possible with the early flowering solandra vine. For covering pergolas, trellis or carports it is difficult to beat a mixture of bignonias (with their large pink, orange, white and yellow trumpet flowers) with a passion flower, bougainvillea and a strong smelling white jasmine. Or again a wisteria can look majestic in the spring. Other possibilities include honeysuckle. However these can probably be put to better use climbing around the trunk of a tree, even allowed to go wild and totally cover the skeleton of a dead tree.

Honeysuckles come in several colours and vigours. Other climbers that can look good in any situation include the clematis, although it needs much watering to survive, and the grapevine. There are several edible varieties available and they can add interest to a garden wall or the trellis work over a patio area.

In addition to adding exotic flowers to the garden, climbers add height and shelter for bird life. Don't be surprised if you attract a few nests.

Climbers can be grown in pots to restrict their growth but they don't look their best and they need frequent watering. They are better planted directly into the ground. But plant them well to stimulate the development of the strong spreading root system necessary for a vigorous growing climber.

First dig over an area of one to two square metres incorporating one or two bucketfuls of well weathered compost or manure. Dig a hole of 50cm diameter and depth, 50cm away from walls and trees as, close in, they tend to be very dry. Fill it with water twice and let it drain away. Add some peat substitute or fine soil to the bottom of the hole. Step on it to firm. Then plant the root ball, infilling and firming until the soil line is just above that of the plant. Support the plant immediately with a stake or tie to the wall, pergola or tree.

As the plant develops tie up and prune to achieve an attractive shape in keeping with the type of climber planted and the location of planting. Remember that some climbers such as the pink flowering bignonia and solandra can grow rampant and get out of control. When planting check the position of your septic tank and outflow. A climber planted close by will soon grow to maturity but in time its roots can block the system. Beware!!

Naturally all climbers need pruning. During the summer cut back any growth that is unsightly or restricts views. Do the main pruning after flowering or in January depending on the flowering season.

25. Colour matching plants

What plants can be grouped together to create harmonised single or related colour beds? Such beds can create dramatic contrasts between adjacent areas of the garden. You may want to cool down a hot sunny area of the garden with greys, whites and blues. Or alternatively warm up a shady area with bright reds, oranges and yellows.

The concept can be used in developing a new garden or in rejuvenating a mature garden in which plants are now past their prime. We consider a number of typical colour combinations. Plants listed were selected on the basis that we know they can do well in the dry Mediterranean climate and soil, provided they are watered during the hot, dry summer months until they are mature. Watering can then be considerably reduced.

A. PLANTS FOR GENERALLY GREEN BEDS OR PATCHES WITHIN CONTRASTING BEDS

1. Green leaves with blue/purple flowers
- ceonothus
- margaritas
- liatris
- hibiscus
- purple lantana
- plumbago
- rosemary
- wisteria

2. Green leaves with white flowers
- camellia
- margaritas
- chrysanthemum frutescens
- lantana
- hydrangea
- viburnum
- jasmine
- bougainvillea
- gardenia
- everlasting candytuft
- heathers

3. Green leaves with yellow/orange flowers
- lantana
- buddleia
- margarita euriopus
- acacia
- broom
- jasmine
- rue
- bignonia
- aeonium (succulent)
- marigolds
- eurios virginiamus
- datura
- hibiscus

4. Green leaves with pink/red flowers
- oleander
- camellia
- pomegranate
- buddleia
- bignonia
- margaritas
- pelargoniums
- aloes
- poinsettia
- heathers
- Judas tree (árbol d'amor)
- lantana

B. PLANTS FOR GENERALLY GREY BEDS OR PATCHES WITHIN CONTRASTING BEDS

1. Grey leaves with blue flowers
Possible plants include
- echium - with pale blue or dark blue flowers.
- sage
- teucreum
- lavender - both the common and officinalis varieties
- globe artichokes

2. Grey leaves with white flowers
- echium
- low growing rockroses
- some irises

3. Grey leaves with yellow /orange flowers
- senecio
- acacia
- santalina
- strelitzia
- potentilla
- stachys byzantina
- low growing gazanias

4. Grey leaves and pink/red flowers
- tamarix
- rockroses
- thyme
- metrosideros
- low growing rockroses
- a number of succulents
- bottlebrush

We hope that the above selections stimulate readers to create new dramatic "cool" or "hot" effects in various corners of the garden. Be courageous and bold! The lists are not intended to be complete, but to be a good starting point. A stroll around a few garden centres will probably suggest others. Some may be new or even rare introductions to the area.

If so check out the following:
- Where were they grown?
- How old are the plants? Have they been forced to their present size or allowed to grow naturally?
- Have they been hardened off from hothouse conditions?
- Do the plants really like our Mediterranean climate or only with copious regular water?

26. Petunias, busy lizzies and fuchsias

Petunias, busy lizzies and fuchsias are three useful summer plants that can flower for months even through to Christmas.

1. PETUNIAS - are a very useful summer plant especially for terraces. With daily watering and weekly feeding, they can flower from February till November/December. In a sheltered spot they may even flower at Christmas. If cut back at the end of flowering, they will often re-shoot and flower for a second year. However, for reliable displays we recommend that new plants be purchased annually. There is a wide range of colours available both in single colours and with stripes.

Plant breeding is resulting in dense, compact plants with larger and larger exotic flowers. However, you can still find the smaller, flowering, trailing varieties in some garden centres. These are particularly useful for window boxes.

If you have green fingers there is a wide range of varieties to be raised from seed. Try the seed tray packs or sow your own seed in a good seed compost, keep covered until they germinate. Pot on when the emerging plants have two or three leaves. Maintain a moist microclimate by placing the pots inside large plastic bags. Prevent rotting off by spraying the soil surface with a natural fungicide or a dilute infusion of horsetail. Whether planted in pots or flowerbeds they can survive in hot sun but they do best in semi-shade. Petunias seem to have few problems. Just water at least every second day, feed weekly and pinch out dying flowers to encourage the continuous production of new buds.

2. BUSY LIZZIES (Impatiens) - are another summer favourite because of their continuous flowering and the wide range of bright colours available. Larger pots of busy lizzies brighten up many terraces, nayas, shady corners and glades in woodland gardens. However, as with petunias, they do best in semi-shade. They need more regular and copious watering than petunias and also respond well to a weekly feed. Busy lizzies can flower through the winter unless hit by frost in the valleys. However, by the New Year they will have become leggy. Stimulate a more compact plant and continuous flowering by trimming the plants. Use the trimmings as cuttings to prepare new plants. Propagate by putting the cuttings in a glass or shallow jar with a centimetre of water or damp cotton wool at the base. Keep in a warm light position. When strong roots develop pot up. When strong plants develop pot on into their final position. Recognise that in full sun they will need watering at least twice a day. If you have the time and memory the effect will be dazzling. For most of us semi-shaded positions are best. In full shade plants become leggy within a few weeks. As with petunias they can be easily grown from seed. A good catalogue such as Chiltern Seeds (telephone: 00 44 1229 5811 37) list an amazing range of colours, single and double flower and 10 cm to two metres high.

3. FUCHSIAS are a third summer favourite for semi-shaded positions. As with petunias and busy lizzies they come in an amazing range of colours. Especially some of the multicoloured varieties. They also come in bushy and hanging formats. Fuchsias have the advantage that they can be grown as hardy perennials or shrubs. However, eventually plants in pots become woody, so take new cuttings annually to keep a constant supply of young plants. Fuchsias can also be raised from seed. A packet of mixed hybrids can produce some very exciting colours. Plants from seed can flower within four to five months

As for care, fuchsias need the following: -

- regular watering
- the removal of dying flower heads to stimulate continual flowering
- trimming to keep to shape - use the trimmings for propagation
- a regular feed and a regular spray against fungi. Use a natural fungicide or a dilute fusion of horsetail.

In the winter many fuchsias lose leaves and look rather unhealthy. Don't lose heart. Trim them to shape and keep just moist. When buds start to show, probably in February or March, start to feed and spray. You will be surprised by their speedy recovery. Cuttings are best taken in the spring or autumn. Break off side shoots. Pinch off the tips and leave four leaves. Dip the cutting in rooting powder and pot up in moist compost. Several cuttings to a pot. Spray with fungicide. Place the pots inside plastic bags, blow up and seal. There will be no need to water until the cuttings have developed good root systems and show signs of new growth. Now remove the plastic and place the pots on a tray of moist soil in the shade when the plantlets have doubled in size re-pot into larger, individual pots they will grow on to flower profusely during the summer months. Re-pot into larger pots in the winter to produce mature plants.

The three plants discussed, petunias, busy lizzies and fuchsias will hopefully give you nine months of colour annually at no great expense.

27. Summer annuals

Annuals can be useful "fill-ins" for both resident gardeners and non-resident owners visiting for the summer months, and also in the autumn and spring. For the latter they are also potentially the means of creating an instant colourful garden. But they are thirsty. They need watering once or even twice a day with good water in hot weather.

1. SELECTION OF PLANTS

First decide on your budget for the purchase and care of annuals. They are not a cheap option when you add up the annual cost of seeds, plants, compost, feed, sprays and water. The alternatives of perennials, shrubs and herbs cost less in the end.

Decide where you wish to plant annuals e.g. in terrace pots, in beds around the front door, around the terrace or pond etc.

Decide on the plant varieties that interest you.

Prepare a planting plan to work out the number of plants you need by variety and colour.

Recognise that groups of similar plants will probably make more impact than individual plants and that close planting will help retain soil moisture and inhibit weed growth.

POPULAR SUMMER ANNUALS PURCHASED BY COSTA GARDENERS

Annuals	Preferred Conditions
Petunias	sun/semi shade
Candytuft	sun/semi shade
Impatiens	shade
Marigolds	sun/semi shade
French Marigolds	sun/semi shade
Portulacas	sun/semi shade
Phlox	sun/semi shade
Stocks	sun/semi shade
Antirrhinum	sun/semi shade
Salvias	semi shade/shade
Zinnias	sun/semi shade
Lavatera	sun/semi shade

If you are not going to be present to water every day, only plant in the shade. You will have less flowers but the plants will survive.

2. PURCHASE OF PLANTS

Purchase strong plants. Plants with good leaf and root growth and plenty of emergent buds.

Unless you need an instant display, for a special event don't buy plants that are in full bloom. The flowers will soon wither and follow on buds will be delayed while the plant concentrates on establishing roots.

Avoid plants with yellowing leaves. If the leaves are starting to rot due to over watering so might the roots.

3. PLANTING

Annuals will not survive unless planted in water-absorbing/retentive soil.

In pots, plant into humus-rich potting compost.

In flowerbeds, dig holes twice as large as the root ball of plants to be planted and work in plenty of potting compost.

Where possible plant in the shade or semi shade versus full sun.

4. WATERING

Without fail water daily. Twice a day if plants are in the sun.

Consider installing a dedicated watering system activated twice a day. A watering system can be run to terrace pots as well as flowerbeds.

Grey water from the kitchen sink can be run to annuals provided you use ecological soap and cleaning products. Keep moist at all times - check for rotting off.

You can obviously use these methods in conjunction with a garden frame and greenhouse.

5. FEEDING

Feed weekly. We suggest a liquid comfrey /manure/nettle feed or a proprietary liquid feed for flowering plants.

6. DEHEADING

Dehead plants as flowers wither. This will stimulate follow on flower buds

With care and attention annuals can flower through the autumn. Petunias and impatiens can flower throughout the winter and survive a second year. After your first year of annuals, ask yourself was the effort and expense worth it? Would it be more effective to plant colourful perennials, cacti, succulents, herbs or shrubs? If you are a lover of annuals, why not raise some from seed next year?

7. RAISING FROM SEED

Annuals can be raised from seed but it is not always easy. Here are a few ideas.

1. Buy seed compost or make a mix of a good light soil and your own friable kitchen compost. If heavy add some sand to improve drainage. You can also use vermiculite if you can find a supplier.
2. Mix in a container and dampen evenly.
3. Use mix to fill any of the following:

a. Polystyrene or plastic seed trays that are divided into small planting holes - about three centimetres square.

b. Polystyrene fish boxes. Make holes in the base for drainage.

c. Small plastic plant pots.

4. Spray with an ecological or proprietary fungicide.
5. Plant seeds thinly according to sowing instructions and relative to the container you use.

For (a) and (b) either cover the whole container in clear plastic and close with clothes pegs to seal, creating a mini microclimate and place in semi shade; or cover with glass and leave in full sun.

Put a three-centimetre layer of damp compost in a polystyrene box (with drainage holes) and stand pots in it, then cover with plastic as above.

Alternatively, if you don't use a box, cover each pot separately with a clear plastic bag and seal. Covering with plastic and sealing creates a mini greenhouse effect. If properly sealed the trays and pots etc., will stay moist and they should not need to be watered while the seeds are germinating.

The benefit of the glass method is that the seeds will germinate much faster. But as soon as the seeds appear you must remove the glass and transfer the containers immediately into a semi-shaded place otherwise they will burn and die. Naturally you can also use a propagator.

8. PLANTING ON

As soon as the seedlings have four leaves, plant on into separate containers until they are strong enough to plant out.

28. Sweet peas

Sweet peas can be sensational in Mediterranean gardens in the spring and early summer. The sweet pea is an annual. There are many varieties and all are best planted in pots or the open ground in the period October to early December. They can also be sown late winter/ early spring but the plants will not flower as early or be as strong to withstand the hot spring sunshine and gusty winds.

Basically they are not difficult plants to grow. But real success will be achieved by paying attention to each of the following nine success factors.

1. Purchase good seeds.

If you browse through most seed catalogues or seed displays you will normally find a few varieties on offer, but generally in a limited number of colours and formats. To achieve a spectacular display it is worth obtaining the catalogue of a specialist grower. We buy new seed from Robert Bolton and Son in the UK (Tel: 00 44 1440 785246 Fax: 788000).

Their catalogue includes many varieties and it is easy to purchase by mail order. Their varieties come in all colours and shades, perfumes and format. They offer both the standard, tall growing varieties and dwarf varieties, particularly useful for mixed beds and flowerpots on the terrace. The shorter varieties are also generally more drought resistant.

2. Prepare plantlets for planting out in March/April as follows:
a. plant in pots in the period October to early December.
b. prepare a good potting mix. As a start try 60 per cent soil, 30 per cent peat and 10 per cent fine sand. If a good loamy garden soil is not available, buy a proprietary seed/potting compost.
c. fill 10 or 15cm pots or boxes with compost. Compact lightly and water. Leave to drain and dry out until the soil is damp but not wet. You can also purchase special plastic planting tubes.
d. plant individual seeds in a circle, two and a half centimetres deep, six to a pot or in rows three to five centimetres apart in boxes. If seeds are hard and dark-coloured, soak them overnight in tepid water. Normally packets indicate whether this treatment is desirable.
e. keep in a warm sunny spot. Once the seeds are through, place in a garden frame or under plastic netting to provide protection from birds, winds and mice. If you have a problem with snails or slugs place comfrey leaves or a proprietary slug killer around the pots.
f. when the plantlets have three pairs of leaves, nip off the top shoot to stimulate the development of a short jointed bushy plant.

3. Decide where you are going to plant out your plantlets in March/April. Prepare the ground by December. Double dig the area and add bone, blood or fish meal fertiliser if you can find it - difficult in Spain. Alternatively dig in well-rotted manure and compost. DO NOT USE FRESH MANURE. Similarly prepare pots ready for planting up.

4. Plant out during a good spell of weather to give newly planted plantlets the chance of getting off to a good start. Dwarf varieties can be grown in mixed beds or pots. The tall growing varieties can be planted to grow through "open" shrubs, to cover the west wall of a shed or house or in rows in the open. This can be either at the back of a large bed or in the vegetable garden. In the latter case, flowers will attract pollinations for flowering vegetables as well as providing cut flowers for the house. But remember that sweet peas will require regular watering and feeding during the growing and flowering seasons. Smaller groups of plants can be supported on wire net tents or vertical cylinders.

Plant the plantlets in two rows, 20-25cm apart and the rows 30cm apart. Stick a sturdy cane in for each plant. Tie the opposite pairs together and to a ridgepole to prevent plants leaning over during heavy rain and winds. Train the plants up the canes tying in with hessian or a soft twine.

If you live in an area where you can grow climbing beans, early plant a few highly perfumed sweet peas between the bean plants. Pollinating insects will be attracted to exactly where they are required. A good example of companion planting that should result in an improved pod set.

5. Keep the plants moist throughout the growing season. Give a good soak to get below the roots once or twice a week rather than a daily top watering that will bring roots the surface. They then scorch and plants weaken, even wither away. Mulch around the plants with damp compost.

6. Feed fortnightly with an organic feed. We find that a diluted comfrey solution plus blood based feed works well.

7. Watch out for aphids. Spray with a soap and water or garlic infusion.

8. Once flowering, pick off the fresh flowers regularly. This will stimulate more flower buds and a longer flowering season.

9. If you want to keep your own seeds for next season, select a strong plant or two and let some of the first flowers go to seed. Pick off the seedpods when dry. Open up the pods and further dry the seeds for a week or two before storing in a labelled airtight container ready for the autumn.

With care and a little luck you should be able to pick sweet peas from May until August.

29. Establishing a herb garden

No Mediterranean garden should be without at least a basic selection of herbs. They never were for the last two millenniums for a number of reasons.

1. Fresh herbs are invaluable for cooking. Perennials such as rosemary, sage, thyme and bay can be freshly picked 365 days a year. Annuals such as dill, parsley, basil and coriander can be cut before they go to seed to use either fresh, for drying or freezing. The seeds can also be gathered just before they ripen and left to dry. Basil can be cut regularly and is also used outside windows and doors to keep flies away.
2. Herb plants are very useful within the flower garden whether planted between annuals, perennials or shrubs, within a rockery or a dedicated herb garden. Herbs offer a wide variety of interesting shapes, colour, flowers, aromas, leaf forms and varied heights.
3. Herbs such as borage and comfrey are very beneficial in enriching the soil and thus creating strong plants. This is important in both the flower and vegetable gardens.
4. Within the vegetable garden companion planted herbs can be very beneficial e.g.
   - rosemary and lavender to attract pollinators.
   - dill, fennel and coriander to attract beetles off vegetables.
   - sage and catmint to deter insects.
5. For organic gardeners other herbs are useful for natural sprays. For instance horsetail infusion to prevent and cure leaf curl on nectarines and peaches. It also prevents mildew on plants.
6. Daily, many people drink herb infusions such as mint, rosemary, fennel, etc., as refreshing caffeine-free drinks rather than tea or coffee.
7. Many herbs are also of benefit medicinally. For instance infusions of: parsley for cystitis; sage for hot flushes and as a mouth wash; mint for digestion and hangovers. And the old age comfrey poultice is still regarded as excellent for speeding up the mending of fractured bones.
8. Many flowering herbs attract butterflies to the garden.
9. And lastly fresh herbs are excellent for natural aromatherapy
   - by brushing against herbs such as rosemary or lavender in the garden.
   - in potpourris, vases or arrangements within the house.
   - bunches of dried herbs in the kitchen.

Luckily herbs not only have these many benefits but most grow well in coastal areas and inland valleys. They do thrive in strong sunshine, high temperatures, poor soil and little water. That is once they are established. Until then they do need regular watering. Also they benefit from close planting and planting amongst rocks to shade roots and stop them drying out. So herbs are a must for most gardens. But "which herbs?" and "where to plant herbs?" As already suggested herbs can be at home in many situations:

-*in pots on the terrace.*
-*scattered between other perennials, shrubs or annuals in flower beds, on rockeries or on terrace walls.*
-*as annual or perennial crops in the vegetable garden.*
-*planted in a formal or semi-formal culinary or medicinal garden close the house.*

The best plants for informal use include sage, thyme, rosemary, oregano marjoram, rue, verbena, lavender and mint. Within a formal herb garden one can easily add parsley, borage, dill, comfrey, tarragon, fennel, coriander, bay and garlic. Most herbs grow reasonably compact. But some such as mint and horsetail have a tendency to put out roots in all directions. It is therefore beneficial to plant them in a sunken pot or old bath to constrain their expansion. Many households use a lot of mint. It can be planted in pots outside the kitchen door but within a year or two it will probably become root bound. So we suggest you repot every winter. Once established most perennial herbs need little treatment except:
- *the occasional pruning to remove dead flowers, to maintain a bush attractive and to stimulate new growth.*
- *each spring a mulch of well rotted compost to feed and reduce water evaporation.*

Herbs such as rosemary, lavender, sage and thyme need little water once established if planted as follows:-
1. Make hole, fill with water, leave to drain, then plant your plant in a well draining but water retentive planting compost.
2. Mulch around plants with compost to help retain moisture.
3. Cover bed with black plastic, making a hole for each plant. The plastic will help keep the ground moist and weeds at bay.
4. Then cover plastic with soil or gravel and stones.
5. For the first few months a drip feed would be beneficial. Other herbs such as parsley, basil and mint are thirsty and need regular watering throughout their lives. They soon become parched in the sun and are often best planted in semi-shady positions.

Indeed several people have commented that they have problems in achieving a perpetual supply of mint in their gardens. Having discussed the problem with them we suggested the following action -

a. *If you grow mint in pots, repot it biannually using a rich well-draining compost. We suggest a 1:1:1 mix of good garden soil, well-rotted manure and gritty sand. Only repot a third of the original root mass into the pot. Use the remainder for two further pots or a patch in the flower garden or vegetable plot. The main problem with mint in pots is that the roots become restricted and instead of spreading sideways they go down. This restricts the continuity of leaves for picking as these grow from spreading runners just below the surface.*

b. *If your mint is planted in the garden, feed it regularly with a liquid comfrey, nettle or manure feed, or a proprietary feed high in nitrogen. This is also of benefit to mint in pots.*

Each autumn mulch the mint patch with well rotted manure or compost when it dies back. Ensure that the mint patch is moist at all times. Mint does not like to dry out. But it does not like clay-like soil. It must have good drainage. You won't find it amongst rosemary and thyme on dry mountainsides.

The autumn is a good time to layout or relayout a herb garden. Perennial plants will be well established by the spring when gaps can be planted with annuals. We find that annual herbs grown from seed germinate best during April and May. Sun loving herbs such as dill, coriander, anis and fennel do well in the full sun. More delicate leafed herbs such as basil and parsley do best in semi-shade. They can be raised first in seed boxes before potting or planting out.

Ask yourself:
Do we use many herbs in our cooking? And for other uses?
Could we use more?
What herbs do we use regularly and occasionally?
What herbs do we buy?
Do we already have them in the garden in sufficient quantity near to the house?
Should we plant more?
What space do we have or could we have for the herb garden?
What would be the most attractive layout?
Why not start preparatory work the next cool day you have?

30. *Perfume in the garden*

Perfume in the garden is very important. The seventh dimension of a successful garden. The other dimensions being layout, vistas, colour, fruit to pick, wildlife and ease of maintenance. Luckily there are many Spanish plants that give out pleasing fragrances or aromas.

We list some of the more popular plants below. This is a basic checklist to help you check out what you have and what to add to enhance your garden before spring and summer.

Fragrant Trees
* orange
* lemon - especially Luna variety
* eucalyptus - dwarf
* philadelphus - mock orange
* mimosas

Fragrant Shrubs
* dama de noche
* lemon verbena
* roses
* datura
* lilac
* pittosporum

Fragrant Climbers
* jasmine - white and pink
* honeysuckle
* roses
* sweet peas
* solandra

Fragrant Herbs
* lavender
* rosemary
* thyme
* mint
* sage

Fragrant Annuals/Perennials
* San Pedro
* scented geraniums
* dwarf sweet peas
* nasturtiums
* stocks

Fragrant Bulbs
* lilies
* fresias
* hyacinths
* alliums
* Spanish/Dutch irises

There are obviously others. Check the smell of the leaves and flowers of plants that look interesting when you walk around garden centres and the gardens of friends. Make a plan of your garden. Mark the direction of the prevailing wind.

Mark up the location of the fragrant plants you have. Consider where and how you could fit in more. Try and place some so that the prevailing wind wafts fragrant perfumes across open doorways and windows, and especially the dining terrace. Wafting perfumes are one of the real joys of dining outside in Spanish gardens. Luckily we can do this for six months or more along the Costas.

So plant some extra fragrant plants ready for summer. Delay the planting of delicate plants until March/April so that they are not affected by cold winds but early enough to be settled in before the hot drying winds that commence in May/June.

31. Roses - Selection and planting

Roses, have been a perennial old favourite in Spain since the days of the Moors. In this chapter we look at the selection of roses and the planting possibilities. Chapter 32 considers the planting and care of young roses. Chapter 33 covers the care of mature roses.

Roses of all types can grow well on the Mediterranean, especially in the cooler inland valleys. For centuries they were favourites in courtyards, walled and formal gardens where they were protected. Over the centuries the choice of rose colour, perfume and habit has become extensive. Year after year amateur and professional plant breeders produce new varieties to choose from. In Spain these are grown locally or imported from specialist growers in northern Europe. If you hunt around you will find nurseries in Spain with a wide selection. If you wait until the autumn or spring to plant, you have the chance of seeing container roses in bloom before making a choice. But first make some basic decisions on how you plan to include roses in our garden.

CHOICE OF HABITS

The following types are available:
- Bush roses that generally grow one to one and a half metres in height. These can be planted in a formal bed or mixed into perennial or shrub beds.
- Standard and half standard roses with stems of approximately 100/120cm and 75/85cm respectively. These can be planted as solitary specimens, in rows along the drive or in the centre of bush roses to give height.
- Climbers and ramblers derived from the original wild roses. As the name suggests they climb in some cases 10 metres or more. Climbers and ramblers can be grown up houses, boundary walls and fences, over internal sheds and walls or even up into and through non-flowering trees to give a special effect. Ramblers can be trained over arches and pergolas.
- Low growing roses are now available that spread quickly and give good ground cover alongside lawns or on banks. They produce a blanket of colour.
- Miniature roses that are grown on special rootstocks for use in patio pots.

CHOICE OF FLOWER

- Hybrid tea roses produce excellent cut flowers. The type one sees in the florist or market stall. The flowers are bred to be perfect specimens that grow singly or in small clusters. The range of colours is now enormous, from deep purple to white with every hue and mix of hues between. In our hot climate the bold colours often give a better display than pastel shades.
- Floribundas are bred to give mass of colour. A mature bush will be almost totally covered with large clusters of flowers when in full bloom. Taller varieties can be used to divide one area of the garden from another. Each flower on a floribunda is generally smaller than a hybrid tea rose
- Then there are the old fashioned roses. Some existed before the plant breeder started to produce the perfect classic rose in the form of the hybrid tea rose. Some are themselves the result of careful or chance breeding. If you want to become a real enthusiast then have a go at cross-pollinating and growing from seed.
- The main old-fashioned roses are musk roses - these grow as rambling bushes up to two metres high but not as climbers. They flower almost continuously during the spring, early summer and autumn. The flowers are generally in cascading clusters.
- Old species roses can be purchased in a number of habits. They can be perpetual flowering, or only flower once or twice a year. Some can be used to create hedges, others a large bush and others foreground cover.
- Renaissance roses - modern cross breeds. Bred especially for their perfume and resistance to disease. Again flower in clusters. Some have large flowers others are perfumed.
- Rugosa roses. These are also useful for hedging or as a large specimen bush.
- Climbers and ramblers climb high. They can be obtained with a wide variety of flowers. Some have a strong perfume.
- Patio climbers have now been bred to be compact and free flowering. Well cared for, they can be covered with small flowers top to bottom.

THE WAY AHEAD

The choice is yours. Don't rush into buying roses visit a few garden centres. Visit a few formal gardens in local towns or the inner gardens of old castles such as in Cordoba. Obtain a few mail order catalogues. But above all decide first whether roses are really for your Spanish garden.

Many of us had excellent rose gardens in northern Europe. Do we want to reproduce our English or Dutch garden or do we want something entirely different? Most importantly recognise that roses need moisture. They will need to be watered throughout the summer, preferably by drip feed. They thrive in full sun but don't like to be wind blown. The roots need a friable, fertile soil with high humus content. The soil needs to be moisture retaining but not one that can become waterlogged. Also roses will not bloom well in the shade. If you decide roses, except for the odd specimen climber, are not for you there are many semi drought-resistant flowering plants to choose from.

32. Roses - Planting and first year care

We continue to look at roses. We give guidance on the purchase, planting and care of roses in the first year after planting.

PURCHASING ROSES

Having made your choice of the types and number of roses to purchase the next task is to seek out strong plants for planting.

There are a number of choices.

- Plants with a good root system in 25 or 30cm containers from a garden centre or nursery.
- Plants in 12 to 15cm plastic pots in supermarkets and garden centre shops. These are often imported. They have been sprayed with a plastic coating to prevent them from drying out and will generally have a smaller root system than plants in large containers. They will therefore need more care in the first year.
- Bare rooted plants from a local grower or mail order. Mail order companies in northern Europe pack plants well and normally give full instructions of what to do on receipt of the plants to ensure that they suffer minimum shock. For winter planting this is an excellent means of purchasing as you can see the strength of the root system you are buying. Our experience is that the specialist growers mail exceptionally strong healthy plants. They cannot risk weak or diseased plants.
- Cuttings can be obtained from prunings of your own or neighbours' favourite roses. Propagating roses is inexpensive and an easy way of producing young rose plants. But naturally you will have to wait two or three years to achieve the mass of flowers of a mature purchased plant.
- Roses can be grown from seed, but this is a long tedious process, and is not practical for most amateur gardeners.

Whichever way you purchase your plants look for the following: -

- Evidence of a strong root system.
- No sign of dead stems or dying back.
- Careful pruning.
- If in leaf, no sign of diseased leaves.
- If in bud, no sign of damaged buds.
- A label indicating the type and colour - it is easy for roses to get mixed up in a busy garden centre.

When you get the plants home keep in a shady cool place and keep them moist until planted.

PLANTING ROSES

1. In a formal bed plant 60 to 75cm apart. In a mixed bed plant so that they are 40 to 50cm from adjacent plants. The roots of climbers and ramblers need more space so plant them two to three metres apart. Likewise with standards to give room for the flowering head to spread and keep separate from the next plant.

2. Dig planting holes to a depth and diameter of 30 to 40cm. Line the hole with a spade of well-rotted manure or compost. Dig in and cover with fine soil. If dry fill the hole with water and let it drain away.

3. Plant container plants so that the union between the main rose stem and rootstock is two to three cm below the soil level. Fill the hole with soil firming level by level. Bring the final level level with the outside soil. When the soil settles it will match the level of the union.

4. If you are planting bare root plants trim the roots to about 25 to 30cm. Spread out the roots as a fan and cover with fine soil, firming level by level as for (3).

5. Water well to ensure that fine soil particles surround all roots and that there are no air holes.

6. Mulch plants with well-rotted manure (horse manure is best), compost or leaf mould and keep moist.

7. The companion planting of a line of roses in the vegetable garden is an excellent way of attracting pollinators for flowering vegetables. Some of the pollinators will also feed on beetles and aphids that attack vegetable plants. The roses will also brighten up the vegetable plot and provide cut roses for the house.

8. If you are rejuvenating an old rose bed, then first remove all plants. Second remove the top 40cm of topsoil. Cover the area with 10cm of well-rotted manure and compost. Dig in and then cover with 35cm of new topsoil.

9. If planting in terrace pots, paint the inside of the pots to prevent evaporation. Then pot up the roses using a potting mix into which you have mixed well-rotted manure or a rose fertiliser.

PRUNING OF NEW ROSES

a. Cut bush roses back to just about the second or third eye above the union.

b. Cut standards back to two or three eyes of the central crown.

c. Climbers and ramblers need no special pruning the first season. Just cut away any shoots that have died back.

FIRST YEAR CARE

1. Feed monthly with manure/comfrey natural feed or with small quantities of a proprietary rose fertiliser to stimulate root and leaf growth.

2. Remove flower buds or flowers as they open.

3. Keep mulched but avoid wood chippings or mushroom spawn. Both can attract disease.

4. Keep moist.

5. If aphids appear, spray with a dilute solution of washing up liquid or crushed garlic.

6. If leaf curl appears, spray with an infusion of horsetail herb or a proprietary spray.

7. If rust appears, remove and burn the leaves and spray as (6).

COMPANION PLANTING TO PROTECT ROSES

Roses can obviously be protected from disease and pests by chemical or organic sprays. However, companion planting can also be very effective. In old cottage gardens ornamental alliums, onions, chives or garlic were planted near roses. Amazingly, garlic does not mask or change the perfume of roses but actually enhances it. The main benefit of the onion family is that they repel aphids in the same way that onions alongside carrots repel carrot flies in the vegetable garden.

A row or pot of parsley alongside roses will help repel rose beetles. An under planting of geraniums or marigolds will help the same way. A row of lupins nearby will help maintain the nitrogen content of the soil. They will also attract earthworms that will move the soil under and around the roots of roses. This will stimulate and maintain healthy roots.

33. Roses - Care of mature plants and propagation

In this chapter we complete the rose story. We give guidance on the care of mature plants.

SECOND AND SUBSEQUENT YEARS PRUNING

1. Roses on the Mediterranean have two flowering seasons. March to July and September to December. In August and January they are generally dormant.

2. Carry out the main pruning in January except in frosty inland valleys. In the valleys delay the pruning until February.

With bush roses prune back to two eyes of the previous year's growth and to shape. Also remove any dead wood, dying back branches and suckers.

Ramblers and climbers need a different treatment. Retain the long strong stems. Cut out weak shoots, dead stems and old flowered stems. Shorten the main stems if plants are becoming too tall or rampant.

3. During the flowering season remove dead flowers and prune back to the next outward-facing bud.

4. At the end of July/early August prune back to strong outward-facing eyes and to shape. Remove inward-growing branches on bushes and standards. This pruning needs to be hard enough to stimulate flower buds for the autumn flowering season.

SECOND AND SUBSEQUENT YEARS CARE

1. Keep well mulched at all times preferably with manure.

2. If you are not able to obtain manure easily then mulch with a peat substitute or grass cuttings and feed the roses in March and May with a proprietary rose fertiliser. It is recommended that roses are not fed once they start to flower.

3. If black spot on the leaves becomes a problem, remove and burn the offending leaves.

4. In December or January spray plants and the earth around with a rose winter wash or solution of Jeyes Fluid. This will reduce the risk of black spot, rust, mildew and leaf curl.

5. If the plants get blackfly or greenfly, spray with a dilute washing up solution, garlic spray or proprietary rose spray.

6. Do not allow roses to dry out.

ROSES FROM CUTTINGS

We are lucky that the Mediterranean climate is excellent for raising roses from cuttings. It is much easier than in Northern Europe. Of the 12 cuttings we planted last February, 10 took successfully and eight were in flower by July. However, we removed the flowers to stimulate the development of strong root systems. This year the young plants will be pruned back to three buds and allowed to flower normally.

To have success with cuttings we suggest the following.
1. When you do your winter pruning keep all healthy prunings that are more than 30cm long and more than the diameter of a Bic biro.

2. Preparing cuttings for planting as follows:
a. Take each cutting and cut the base just below a leaf joint. Then cut the top just above a leaf joint to produce cutting approximately 25 to 30cm in length.
b. Cut a one to two cm slit in the bottom of the cutting and insert two dry sweet corn kernels.
c. Remove all leaves except the top two if they are still green.
d. Push into the ground in your planned final position, or pot six to a 25cm plastic flower pot in a sandy potting compost, or make a V-trench in an out of the way part of the garden and plant the cuttings half their depth and 15 to 20cm apart. Fill the trench with a sandy potting compost.
e. Mulch the cuttings with well-rotted manure or compost. Water just enough to stop the cuttings from drying out.
f. When the cuttings have produced new leaves, feed monthly with a comfrey or proprietary rose feed to stimulate the development of the root system.
g. If the cuttings bud and flower remove them to stimulate the plants to use all their energy developing a root system.
h. After 12 months plant out the strongest cuttings to your planned final position in the flower or vegetable garden.
i. From then onwards treat as a purchased plant.

Naturally you can plant cuttings at any time of the year. They are free so why not have a go. But generally one will be more successful if cuttings are planted during October/November or February/March.

34. Camellias

A very traditional Spanish shrub. A shrub that can develop into a spectacular specimen within just a few years. They can be grown in large earthenware pots or tubs, or in sheltered, shady beds in the garden.

PURCHASING PLANTS

Camellias are best purchased between February and April. There are several flower forms and a wide range of single or dual-coloured flowers - whites, pinks, creams and reds. Camellias are sometimes not that well labelled in garden centres. So purchase when plants have one or two opening buds. You can then check the flower format and colour. If possible do not select plants that have most of the buds already open. If you do the flowers will drop quickly, as the newly planted bush concentrates on settling in its root system. If you purchase and plant a shrub with only a few buds showing colour, you have a good chance of spectacular flowers over a six to eight week period during the first spring.

As well as looking for a plant with plenty of healthy flower buds, also look for a plant with large, shiny leaves and a good balanced branch structure. Avoid unbalanced plants and those that have a large number of yellowing or dry leaves. This probably indicates that the plant has suffered from a recent period of over or under watering.

CARE OF PLANTS

Having purchased strong, well-shaped, healthy plants they will now need careful planting and ongoing care.

1. Plant in a friable, acid soil. A soil full of humus. If your natural garden soil is neutral, alkaline or just acid, purchase a bag of acid plant compost such as used for azaleas. Use this to pot up in terrace pots and fill a large planting hole in the garden. Camellias can do very well in the semi-shade beneath the pine trees, as the soil will be naturally acid. Mulch well with well-rotted compost or manure after planting.

2. Camellias do not like to be under or over watered, especially in the first few years when the root structure is developing. Whenever possible water with rainwater or natural spring water. They do not thrive with highly chlorinated water.

3. Plant or place pots in a shady or semi-shady spot. Potted shrubs are best kept on the north or west aspect of the house for most of the year, away from heavy winds and rains.

Potted plants can be moved to the semi-shade of a south, east or west facing naya each spring for the flowering season. Move the pots back to a shaded/semi-shaded position on the north side of the house or wooded part of the garden when the flowers have fallen. Don't forget to water the dormant plants twice a week in the hot weather.

4. The only other attention required is:
* An autumn feed to stimulate new flower buds.
* A very occasional pruning to shape into a balanced bush.

Looked after well they will grow into very impressive tall shrubs.

Newly purchased plant

Plant a month later

35. Flowering trees

Flowering trees are very important in the garden. The flowers add colour and in many cases a heavy perfume. Some trees are impressive for their mass of flower and others for impressive individual flowers. The choice is enormous.

Flowering trees have a place in island beds or terraces and also along the boundary. Here they can add shape, height and interest to an otherwise monotonous stretch of hedging, shrubs and walls. The following selection would add colour during nine months of the year. Naturally the flowering time will vary by a few weeks depending on your exact location in Spain.

TREE	FLOWER COLOUR	FLOWERING PERIOD
1. Mimosa	yellow	Jan/April
2. Almond	pink/white	February
3. Apricot	pink	February
4. Pear	white	Feb/March
5. Judas	reddish pink	Mar/April
6. Lemon (Luna)	white	Every 6/8 weeks
7. Orange	white	Mar/April
8. Oleander	white/pink/red	April/December
9. Jacaranda	blue	May/June
10. Mimosa	yellow/pink	June/July
11. Schinus (Pepper tree)	yellow	June/July
12. Devils Tongue (Lengua Diablo)	yellow/red	July/August
13. Jupiter Tree	pink/red	August/September

Whenever you decide to plant trees, plant them well. First dig a planting hole three times the width and two times the depth of the existing root ball. Fill the hole with water and let it drain away twice. Then fill the bottom of the hole with a mixture of peat substitute and soil, adding a handful of bonemeal or shovelful of well rotted garden compost. Tread this down. Now knock in a support stake. Then place the root ball in the hole loosening up any compacted root mass. Tie the trunk to the support stake using wire threaded through a short length of garden hose. This will prevent damage to the bark. Then fill the hole firmly adding compost to the soil as you go. Firm down the top and make a watering moat 90cm from the trunk. Make sure that new trees are not allowed to dry out. Put them on a drip feed or water deeply every few days.

Mulching, the adding of a protective layer of vegetable matter around trees and shrubs, is beneficial for three reasons. Five to 10 centimetres of mulch material will help prevent water evaporation, stop weeds from developing and in time enrich the soil. Garden worms will gradually work the rotting vegetable matter into the soil adding vital humus and minerals.

Useful mulches include garden compost, cardboard or newspapers covered with grass cuttings, well-rotted manure mixed with other materials such as peat substitute and wood chippings. However wood chippings do tend to attract woodlice that can attack roots. Once in the soil they are difficult to eradicate.

As a substitute for vegetable material, five centimetres of stone chippings on top of perforated plastic sheet can look attractive. They are very effective in retaining moisture and preventing weeds, but they will not improve the quality of the soil.

April jacaranda

36. Palms

A single group of mature palms can look majestic and exotic. Even when small they achieve an immediate Mediterranean effect. But their selection planting and maintenance needs to be done well.

Palm trees offer several benefits.
1. They can grow into impressive elegant specimens capable of growing safely for several hundred years.
2. There are more than 50 varieties available - but not all are readily available on the Costas.
3. They look good as a small oasis or as freestanding specimens. There are tree and shrub varieties.
4. They can add valuable shade around the pool, on the lawn or along the driveway to shelter the car.
5. When established they can withstand drought conditions and gales.
6. The roots do not spread extensively. They are not thirsty water-seekers like eucalyptus. They can therefore be planted only a few metres from the pool or septic tank. But take care!

Naturally there are a few risks.
1. If a pool or septic tank has leaks then any roots will seek them out - and palm roots are thick and strong.
2. The trunk of a palm thickens annually. On some palms it can expand from 20cm in diameter to a metre or more in 10 years. Holes in terraces and distances from paths and walls need to be considered carefully.

3. Mature palms have a heavy umbrella of branches. They can take the sun and views away from windows and other parts of the property.

4. Tall palms are difficult to prune and they need an annual pruning to stay healthy and look good. An un-pruned palm can become top heavy and dangerous.

5. Palms do attract fungal diseases; they need to be inspected regularly. A toppling palm is dangerous to property and people.

6. As palms get bigger be careful of their spikes near the trunk (at eye level or head level). Keep this in mind when you choose your planting place i.e. not too close to pathways.

SELECTING PALMS

The most commonly available palms are listed below:
MATURE HEIGHT

Tall (8-20m):	Washingtonia Robusta; Trachycarpus Excelsa; Cocus Plumosa; Phoenix Dactylifera; Phoenix Canariensis; Chamerops Excelsa.
Med. (5-8m):	Syagrus Romanzoffianum; Phoenix Roebelenii; Lewtonia Australis; Chamerops.
Short (3-5m):	Butia Capitata; Chamerops Humilis; Livingstonia Chinensis; Sabal Palmetto.

Recognise that the heights attained will depend on the quality of plant you buy, how well you plant it and its ongoing care.

Choose a type of palm that adds shape and beauty to your garden when young and mature. Visit palm gardens before making a final decision.

Recognise that palms can also be grown from seed. Seed will be found below any mature fruiting palm. Chiltern seeds (Tel: 00 44 1229 581137) Fax: 584549) offer a mix of rare palm seeds from the Dominican Republic that would probably grow in our climate.

Plant some now. Your children and grandchildren may enjoy the benefits.

A young palm from seed

PLANTING PALMS NEEDS CARE

Palms are expensive to purchase. They can grow tall and indeed they may be several metres high when first planted. They therefore deserve care during planting to ensure that: -
- the palms are held firmly in the ground.
- the roots are stimulated to grow to anchor the palm and search for water and nutrients.
- the branches are protected from sun and wind until established.

The best time for planting, as for all large trees and shrubs, is October to February. Earlier or later will require daily watering.

Having decided where to plant your selected palms, dig a hole the depth of the root-ball and slightly wider than the container or loose root-ball. The soil mark on the stem of the purchased palm should be level with the soil on either side of the hole once planted.

Next fill the hole with water and allow it to drain away. This may take several hours. If water does not drain away in two hours loosen the soil in the bottom of the hole. If no improvement, consider planting elsewhere. Palms are suited to dry conditions, so you don't want them waterlogged.

PLANTING

Medium and large palms need the branches tying up to prevent the branches drying out and to stop the roots moving too much. Tie them up securely inside a piece of sacking or hessian beach mat. Smaller palms can just be tied with string. This will need to be left in place during the first year.

Loosen the soil at the bottom of the dug hole. Dig in well-rotted manure or compost. Incorporate a few comfrey leaves. Cover with soil and firm.

Carefully remove the root-ball of the palm from its container or sack. Ensure that the root-ball is kept as intact as possible. Loose roots are likely to dry out.

Lower the root-ball into the hole. This may need two people or even a crane for a large specimen. Fill the hole surrounding the root-ball with a crumbly rich soil. A 3:1 soil rotted manure mix is ideal. Fill the soil to halfway, firm and water in. Repeat until the hole is full and firm up to the surrounding soil area.

With tall palms support the palm trunk with tie-ropes or wooden struts. These will need to be left on for up to two years.

Do not allow the soil to dry out for the first year and until the green top shows sign of new growth.

Then remove the protective covering and fan out the branches.

ONGOING CARE

Palms should only need watering during long periods of drought. They need little feeding but benefit from an annual mulch of well-rotted manure or compost. Palms need a good annual pruning to remove dead branches, flowers and fruiting stems. Be careful to avoid the long sharp spikes on many species, they are easily pruned when young and short but more difficult when the palm tree rises above house level and beyond the reach of the normal household ladder. Town halls have no problems as they can employ professionals able to climb the trunks safely on high platform turntables. The safest thing is for private persons to also employ a professional. A well-pruned palm head will look like a pineapple. Sadly many tall trees look neglected with years of dead branches hanging down.

Side-shoots often grow from female trees. These become unsightly and should be cut off close to the trunk. Such cuttings can be potted up in large pots or planted in a damp sheltered spot to produce new young palms.

An untrimmed palm

Palm cuttings are difficult to rot down. They also take a long time to burn on a bonfire. It is therefore best to cut them up into one-metre pieces and take to the local tip. (Keep the pieces cut off nearest to the trunk that are dangerously sharp in a separate pile and handle very carefully.)

A better pruned palm

37. Cacti

The cacti family is very useful in Mediterranean gardens for a number of reasons. They are very drought resistant and come in a wide range of forms, colours, type of flower and height. Inexpensive small plants and expensive giant specimens are widely available. They can also be raised from cuttings, runners or seeds.

Cacti can look good in pots, on rockeries, in dedicated cacti beds or gardens, or as individual specimens in appropriate parts of the garden. In general although prickly they are not poisonous

1. TYPES OF CACTI AVAILABLE

There are several hundred varieties of cacti. Before you make any decisions on the type, number and layout we suggest you visit specialist cactus gardens in your area.

The following are among the cacti most popular and easily grown.

Opuntia	- the prickly pear family. There are several forms. Some growing huge and others relatively small.
Echino cacti	- rounded and very prickly.
Cereus	- tall and branching, almost like trees in format.
Dracaena	- can grow quickly as tall columns with branches.
Agaves	- with long arching green, yellow or variegated leaves. Eventually grow to two metres high with a tall spectacular flower.
Aloes	- recognised by their fleshy leaves, woody stems and erect spikes of orange, red or yellow flowers. The juice in the leaves is called aloe and is used extensively in natural medicine and cosmetics. The most popular varieties are Aloe Vera, native to West Indies and Cape from South Africa. They prefer unchlorinated water and indirect sunlight.

For the purist the latter two are succulents and not cacti. However we include them as they look like and blend in with cacti.

Most cacti in Mediterranean gardens flower annually, intermittently or only once in their lifetime. Flowers may last for a week or only a matter of hours, or perhaps into the middle of the night.

Most can cope with the coastal climate but some would be too tender for the winter frosts experienced in inland valleys.

2. PURCHASING OF CACTI

- Decide where you want to plant cacti and whether in the ground or in containers.
- Draw up a planting plan and make a list of the varieties, colours, sizes and the number of each required.
- Look for plants with healthy plump leaves and good root systems.

3. PLANTING OF CACTI

Cacti thrive best in a well draining sandy soil. For pots and planting in the garden prepare a planting compost of equal parts of coarse sand or grit, compost and soil. A handful of finely broken up old mortar or old pots to each litre of compost will ensure good drainage. Also if you have charcoal left over from barbecues, break it up and place at the bottom of pots or planting holes to provide drainage and to keep the soil around the roots sterile.

Firm root balls firmly but tenderly. Mulch with coarse sand and fine stone chippings.

4a. WATERING

The basic rules are as follows.
1. Use rainwater or well water rather than chlorinated water.
2. Water around the roots not over the plants.
3. Don't over water as roots can rot. Cacti don't like to be continuously wet.
4. In general just give the occasional water in winter if very dry, and water more regularly in the hot summer months of June to August. Pot plants will benefit from an occasional light spray from Sept/March. Mature plants with deep taproots will need less watering than small plants in pots that can dry out quickly.
5. In summer it is best to water pots well from the base and then do not water again until they have been dry for a few days.

4b. FEEDING

Cacti welcome an occasional feed during the flowering summer months. Use a special cacti feed or a dilute mix of liquid manure, comfrey and nettles.

5. PROPAGATION

In general cacti are easy to propagate by taking cuttings or removing offsets. Before planting, leave them to dry for a few days until a hard callus forms over the cut. With varieties such as the Opuntia prickly pears, just cut off a leaf and most will take. With more delicate types such as the Schlumbergera and Christmas Cactus, remove cuttings at the joints and plant up.

Cacti soon root. Rooting powder can however speed the process of developing a good root ball. Cacti can also be raised from seed. But this is something for the cacti specialist, as it requires care and attention over a number of years. With the wide variety of inexpensive young cacti available, it is not worthwhile for most.

Keep all potted cuttings in a good light and water sparingly. Remember that their natural homelands are deserts or semi-deserts.

6. STIMULATING FLOWERS

* Less frequent watering encourages more flowers.
* Bright hot conditions are required by most. However the Christmas Cactus benefits from being put in a dark cupboard from 17.00-8.00 from early November until the first flowers appear.

7. CLEAN UPS

* Remove any rotting leaves.
* As agaves grow, saw off lower leaves to keep them in shape.

8. CONTROLLING PESTS

* If you do have a problem with cacti becoming soft and rotting spray all plants in the area with a fungicide.
* Mealy bugs can be a problem. Remove with a stick and spray with a fungicide to kill off the remainder and prevent them spreading. However most cacti will be disease free.

9. DANGERS

We understand that most cacti are non-poisonous although they have a reputation for being so.
Beware of prickly ends, the many spikes and itching hairs.
The main precautions to be taken are: -
a. Cut off offending ends.
b. Plant away from main pathways.
We hope that if your soil and situation is ideal you manage to emulate one of the specialist cactus gardens over the next decade.

38. Hedges - boundary and internal

Good hedges give valuable privacy from passers-by and the neighbours. And when established, an excellent alternative to a two metre wall or fence. The latter being expensive to build and forbidden by bylaws on some urbanisations.

Within a garden, internal high hedges can provide a screen and windbreak around the pool, barbecue/eating areas, the vegetable plot and washing line area. Lower hedges can provide interesting transitions from one part of the garden to another.

Combining both high and low hedges, one might create a number of mini gardens each with a unique design, plants, colour and microclimate.

So what are the reliable possibilities for hedges?

1. BOUNDARY HEDGES

1.1 Thick Screens
a. Cupressus
b. Pittosporum
c. Laurel/Bay
d. Gandula/myporum
e. Privet
f. Berberis
g. Ivy

1.2 Less Dense Screens
a. Oleanders
b. Hibiscus
c. Bougainvillea

1.3 Open Screens
a. Rambler roses
b. Bignonias
c. Prickly pear cacti

2. INTERNAL HEDGES

2.1 High
As above plus
a. Honeysuckle
b. Jasmine
c. Plumbago
d. Passion flower

2.2 Low/Medium
a. Hibiscus
b. Lavander
c. Lantana
d. Rosemary
e. Berberis
f. Buddleia
g. Box
h. Ceonothus
i. Rock roses.

In all cases select strong bushy plants. Dig a 50cm by 50cm trench. Line the bottom with a 1:1 mix of good soil and well-composted manure. Plant and fill in firmly with a good loamy soil. Stake plants if necessary or tie in to a post and wire. Water in well and regularly until established - probably two or three years depending on your local conditions. A timed drip system would be a good idea.

One of the problems on the Costa, especially in new urbanisations, is that people want an instant two metre high hedge. They purchase and plant two metres plus tall cupressus and fail to recognise the amount of watering and support required for two or even three years before they have a strong deep root structure. Last year we saw such a hedge planted by professional contractors. The plants were leggy for their height. They would have been much bushier at two metres if they had been planted as one-metre or 50cm plants two or three years earlier. Each plant was staked with a two-metre cane with canes tied across, each plant being tied to the canes. A month later and again six months later, the cane frame was a mess. Trees leant in all directions. Half the canes came out of the ground and many of the wire ties broke.

Remember coastal and valley winds can reach 80 to 100kms an hour on the Costa, and can come from all directions. There are six reliable rules for planting cupressus. Plant small. Plant deep. Stake with good posts a metre into the ground. Use strong cross wires and tying wires. Water well. Reinforce with canes threaded through and securely tied.

39. Establishing wildlife in the garden

Much can be done to introduce and attract wildlife into the garden. The benefits being as follows:
- Adds interest
- Attracts pollinators
- Attracts bug eaters
- Provides an ecological haven

The latter much-needed with the continuing cutting down of hedges and copses, infilling of ponds and barrancos and the ever-increasing number of commercial and residential estates.

The winter is a good time to take action before hibernating animals, insects and migratory birds reappear. The following 13 actions are our favourites. Each is practical and not excessively expensive or time consuming.

1. Install a number of bird boxes fixed to sheltered high walls or mature trees. If possible fix near or within leaf cover. Also fix at a height difficult for cats to jump or climb to. Purchase or make bird boxes with a variety of sizes and holes. A small four-centimetre circular hole for long-tailed tits and a larger eight-centimetre hole for hoopoes. Put a pile of straw in a corner of the garden as nest building material.

2. Fix a bat box under the eves. It may take a few summers before it attracts a family of bats, but it is worth waiting. Fix the box so that the opening can be seen from the terrace on a balmy summer evening.

3. Build a mound of leaves and twigs a metre cubed in a hidden corner of the garden. Don't disturb it or use the pile for compost. With luck you will attract a pair of hedgehogs. It will also attract worms and a selection of insects. Field mice might also make the pile their home.

4. After cutting down a tree or large branches, leave a pile of logs in a quiet corner. Again a variety of insects will be attracted that provide food for the birds. You might also attract a pair of large, black smooth snakes, which can grow to one and a half metres. But watch out that you don't attract dangerous adders.

5. Build a self-standing or hanging bird table. Ensure it has an edge to stop food blowing off and to provide a perch for the visiting birds. Place a mixture of nuts, seeds, fatty scraps and a bowl of water on the table. These will attract and help semi-tame a variety of wild birds. Avoid chunks of dry bread as they could swell up in the stomachs of birds. They are particularly dangerous to young birds. As in Northern Europe, many Mediterranean gardens, including our own, have a resident winter robin. Cut back the feed on the table in summer so that birds eat unwanted pests.

6. Purchase a birdbath and place in a prominent position. Keep topped up with clean, unchlorinated water.

7. Purchase a few coconuts, break and hang a few halves around the garden. Attach them to branches of trees about two metres above ground level. Position them so that they can be seen from the naya and windows. They attract a variety of tits all year round. You can also hang up nets of peanuts.

8. Sow some sunflower seeds in pots in March and plant them out when 20cm high. Tie a cane to give support and to remind you where they are while young. The open flowers will attract a variety of pollinators. Leave a few ripe heads on the tall stems through the winter. A variety of seed-eating birds will be attracted.

9. Prepare an area of the garden, perhaps a bank or corner of the orchard, for planting a mix of wild flower seeds in April or May. Left wild, many will self-seed the following year. The patch will not only give a blaze of colour but also attract butterflies and other pollinators.

10. Leave a corner of the lawn or orchard uncut. Allow wild flowers to develop. A variety of insects including grasshoppers and butterflies can be attracted. This is only feasible if you have a good water supply.

11. Winter is a good time to dig out a pond. This can be lined with a thick plastic sheet if you want a quick and less expensive pond than one built with concrete and reinforcing steel mesh. If you have the space build a pond double the size you initially think of. Aquatic plants, especially water lilies grow very quickly. They cover the surface area so that fish cannot be easily seen and their root masses soon restrict the volume of water available for the fish to swim freely. Within a couple of years a pond built now will probably provide interest from frogs, toads, damsel and dragonflies. There is a wide variety of pond fish to choose from that thrive in the mild Mediterranean climate.

12. Consider including a small bog garden on a ledge in the pond. Again there are a variety of plants that will soon settle and mature. A mix of irises can be visually attractive and will also provide a sheltered haven for frogs and toads.

13. If you are building new terrace walls leave a few holes with cavities behind. With luck toads, which devour many unwanted garden bugs, will settle.

Naturally, all the above actions are in addition to designing and developing a garden with a good variety of flowering, perfumed perennials, shrubs and trees.

40. *Attracting butterflies*

Butterflies can add much beauty to Mediterranean gardens. They have been called "flying flowers" and also are good pollinators. Some gardens have swarms of several hundred butterflies flitting around on a hot summers day and others nearby merely the occasional passing visitor.

So what can you do to attract and retain more butterflies? Put simply you need to plant plants that provide food for butterflies and caterpillars, and plants on which butterflies will lay eggs. What does that mean in practice? Butterflies within Mediterranean gardens include swallowtails, fritillaries, tortoiseshells, red admirals and a wide variety of browns, yellows, blues and whites. All need a continuous supply of easily accessible nectar on which they feed. Nectar can be best provided by having masses of bright coloured fragrant flowers with a flat open petal format. Flat open flowers make it easy for butterflies to extract nectar. Favourite flowers include lantanas, margaritas, marigolds, ice plants, herbs and the purple buddleia. The purple buddleia is a specially powerful magnet but the more subtle yellow and pink varieties perform poorly. Although a moth rather than a butterfly the fascinating humming bird hawk moth loves to hover in front of deep throated flowers such as the devil's tongue (lengua diablo) and honeysuckle.

Plants attract most when planted in groups to create a mass of flowers rather than isolated plants. And most importantly they need to be in full sun. You will notice that few butterflies stay in the shade or fly around on dull days.

Different plants are required to stimulate butterflies to lay their eggs in your garden and to provide food for caterpillars. If your garden is surrounded by uncut meadows or natural mountainsides such plants probably exist naturally just over the wall.

But for most of us urbanisations have decimated natural habitats:

We therefore need to take some of the following corrective actions.

a. Develop a wild corner of the garden. Best is an uncut area of meadow, orchard or lawn.

b. Plant up pots with tall grasses, thistles and stinging nettles. Cut back a third of the latter monthly to maintain a continuous stream of young shoots and leaves. The pots can be easily hidden among other plants in sunny positions.

c. Plant the blue coloured scabious in flowerbeds, pots or wild grassland.

d. Grow honeysuckle up sunny walls or old tree trunks.

e. Plant a herb corner including marjoram, lavender and thyme.

f. Plant an area of decorative cabbages and accept that they will be nibbled by caterpillars particularly the large cabbage whites.

Rarely will caterpillars be in sufficient numbers to create a noticeable nuisance even in the vegetable garden. It is important to provide dark shelter for hibernating butterflies and chrysalises. Shade can be provided by ivy clad walls or fences, exposed tree roots, piles of rocks or logs, an open garden shed or log shed, old seats etc.

A selection of the above actions could start to have an impact within a year. But remember that success and failure is also very dependent on the weather. Three summers ago we had several hundred recently hatched butterflies fluttering from flower to flower for several days. An hour's heavy thunderstorm drowned them all. We never saw more than three or four butterflies during the rest of the summer.

If you are really interested in "flying flowers" we suggest that you borrow or buy a specialist book on Mediterranean butterflies.

41. Establishing a wilderness corner

Many gardeners have the possibility to develop part of the garden into a natural wilderness corner. An ecological protected area that encourages natural plants and grasses to take over profusely.

The benefits are fivefold:

1. The brightening up of an otherwise dull, perhaps almost impossible part of the flower garden, lawn or orchard.
2. The creation of a colourful spring feature. Many wild flowers bloom before beds of cultivated annuals, perennials and shrubs are at their peak.
3. The preservation of varieties of natural wild flowers and grasses that may become rare as more and more land is built on and the use of garden and agricultural chemicals expands.
4. The creation of a small nature reserve. Many wild plants attract birds, butterflies, small mammals and insects.
5. An area of the garden that will require less water per square metre per annum than most other areas.

In theory a wild plant can be grown as well as cultivated plants. But in practice it is not that easy. Each variety needs the right conditions. And the conditions vary widely.

TYPICAL LOCATIONS

There are three typical locations for wild or wilderness areas.
A. A semi shady part of the lawn or orchard.
B. A stony embankment or slope.
C. A rocky hillside.

The three locations each offer different possibilities and problems. The objective in each case is to create an area as natural as possible that contrasts with other areas of the garden, with minimum preparatory or maintenance effort at low expense. In this chapter we deal with locations A and B. C is discussed separately in Chapter 45 - Constructing a rockery.

Before deciding on what type of location to develop drive around local lanes, agricultural valleys and the inner valleys, especially between May and June. Study the motorways - when a passenger! You may be amazed by nature's natural colour and aroma effects just a kilometre or so from the Costa. Even on the shady side of sand dunes. The challenge is to replicate the best you see. It won't be easy. But the effect will be worth the patience.

A. ENCOURAGING A WILD MEADOW

The end of the lawn or an area of an orchard can often be encouraged to become colourful meadowland particularly if semi shaded for most of the day. If you let the lawn go uncut for a month you will probably already see signs of wild flowering plants, particularly if you don't use lawn chemicals.
So what action needs to be taken?

1. Stop using chemical weed killers or fertilizers on or near the chosen area.
2. Allow the area to grow naturally through to September.
3. Allow any flowering plants and grasses to flower, seed and die back naturally. Yes some will be weeds. But so were useful herbs and bedding plants before their properties were discovered to be beneficial and seed men and plant breeders took over from nature.
4. Collect ripe seeds from your own garden and from the countryside. Don't collect plants. They probably won't take and in some cases it will be illegal.
5. Watch for the availability of Spanish wild flower seeds in seed catalogues and seed displays. Packets of northern European wild flowers will normally not be suitable for our climate unless you have a damp microclimate around a spring or river up in the valleys.
6. Cut existing grass/plants in September. Remove all the cuttings. From now on starve rather than feed the soil.
7. In September or October aerate the area and spread a centimetre of poor soil over it. Brush into aerated holes.
8. Sow the seeds of flowers, plants and grasses by scattering over the surface. Either sow in dedicated patches of individual plants or colours or intermix all together. Try sowing in September/October and in February/March. Initial seeds could include poppies, dill, fennel, salvia, scabious, silenes, clavels, clover, wild lupins, thistles, wild garlic, buttercups, San Diego de noche and lavatera.
9. Sieve a fine sand/poor soil mix over the seeds and firm.
10. If you plan a dense sowing of mixed wild flowers and grasses we suggest you make a number of successive sowings over a period of three or four weeks in an attempt to match the optimum sowing conditions. Some seeds will come up in the autumn and some in the spring.
11. Keep the newly sown area damp but not wet. In this way you should achieve a higher germination rate than in nature.
12. You can also raise seeds in pots or boxes as you would annuals for later planting out.
13. Just leave the area to grow wild. Cut the grass each autumn. Hay making would be earlier and twice in the lush meadows of northern Spain, but on the hot Costas use the grasses to protect roots during the summer.
14. Don't waste summer water on the area.

B. CREATING A FLOWERING BANK

The creation of a colourful bank will require the replication of the natural microclimate found along sun baked roadsides, motorways and the edge of fields. For the best chance of success:

1. Choose a semi shaded bank.
2. Check that the bank, whether natural or created by the dumping of builders' rubble, is reasonably friable and well draining when wet and not a solid lump of clay. The latter would squeeze and strangle roots when dry.
3. A mature bank will have had years of natural soil enrich-

ment as the result of dying vegetation being taken into the soil by worms and ants. So mix in some compost and dried grass to the top few inches, mixed with some sand or fine chippings.

4. Plant seeds that thrive on banks. Try poppies, wild sweet peas, broom, antirrhinums, milamores, lupins, marigolds, thistles, buddleia and wild garlic. Recognise that many seeds will fail. Banks of poppies drop thousands of seeds but fail to produce flowering plants. Try an autumn and spring sowing.

5. Dampen the bank after sowing and keep damp until emergent plants are established.

6. Just leave the bank to become wild. Only cut back in the autumn if it becomes very luxuriant and grasses start to take over the flowers. Hopefully you will have a colourful meadow or bank within two or three years, rich in wildlife as well as preserving Mediterranean plants.

42. Garden bulbs

There is a wide variety of bulbous plants that will do well on the Costas, coming in a wide variety of single and multicolours, and heights from a few centimetres to a metre or more. They can brighten up flowerbeds, rockeries and, in pots, any corner of the terrace or naya.

The bulbous family includes all those plants we refer to as bulbs (e.g. tulip), corms (e.g. gladioli) and rhizomes (irises).

We consider what to plant, how to plant and how to generally care for mature bulbs.

1. WHAT CAN BE PLANTED?

The following list summarises the most popular. The selection of bulbous plants on the Costa is often limited. Wider choices will be available in the UK and Holland. We suggest you look around when travelling north in the summer and early autumn or ask summer visitors to bring you supplies. There are many others available from specialist suppliers, particularly in Holland and South Africa.

Plant	Colours generally available	Typical flowering Times	Best Planting Times
Agapanthus	Blue/White	June/July	Autumn
Aliums	Various	June/Aug	Autumn/Spring
Alstroemeria	Various	June/Dec	Autumn
Amaryllis	Various	Dec/Mar	Autumn
Anemone	Many	Dec/Feb	Autumn
Arium Lily	White/yellow	Mar/Apr	Autumn
Canna	Many	June/Aug	Spring
Clivia	Yellow/red	Feb/Apr	Autumn
Crocus	Various	Dec/Feb	Autumn
Daffodil	White/yellow/orange	Jan/Apr	Autumn
Freesia	Various	Jan/Mar	Autumn
Gladioli	Many	June/July	Spring
Grape Hyacinth	Blue/white	February/March	Autumn
Hyacinth	Various	February/March	Autumn
Irises	Various	February/March	Autumn
Lilies	Many	April/June	Autumn
Oxalis	Various	May/June	Spring
Ranunculus	Various	February/May	Autumn
Tulip	Many	March/April	Autumn

The flowering times will vary according to the shelter and height of your garden, the time of planting and winter rainfall.

2. PLANTING

- Planting depths range from 10cm for crocus to 30cm for lilies. Follow the planting instructions on the packet but generally plant deeper than you did in Northern Europe.
- Plant in single colour groups for effect.
- Plant specimen amaryllis and agapanthus in pots for terrace displays. Allow to die back after flowering and feed when new growth appears.

- Pot up bulbs in September or October for a Christmas display. Place in a dark cellar or garage to accelerate their growth. Bring out from the beginning of December to stimulate the forming buds to swell and flower.

3. FEEDING

- If the soil is poor, enrich by digging in some compost at the time of planting.
- Fertilise in the spring when the tops first break the soil, with a potash-rich fertiliser or well-rotted manure to stimulate better flowers and reproduction.

4. WATERING

- Spring flowering bulbs in the ground will only need watering in very dry weather. But it will prolong flowering times. Water at the base, not over the flowers.
- Bulbs in pots will require regular watering as they dry out.
- Summer flowering bulbs will need regular watering once above the ground to stimulate leaf growth, flowering and reproduction.

5. PROBLEMS

- Our experience is that hard skinned corms and rhizomes survive better than soft skinned bulbs on the Mediterranean. Plants such as Spanish irises, cannas and freesias multiply year after year with no trouble. But daffodils, hyacinths, tulips and lilies planted in the garden suffer big losses after flowering the first year. During the hot summer months the succulent flesh of the bulbs are attractive and easy to reach foods for slugs and a variety of insects. It is therefore best to dig up fleshy bulbs after drying off after flowering. Dry them and store ready for autumn planting.
- Summer corms like cannas won't flower unless kept well watered.

6. GROWING FROM SEED

- With our hot spring and summer climate try bulbous plants from seed. Start with freesias which even self-seed freely.

7. PROPAGATION BY SPLITTING

- Separate blocks of irises and agapanthus every few years and use the smaller outside plantlets for planting up new areas or expanding existing patches of plants.

43. Garden pond - construction

A formal or informal pond can be a fascinating feature in both large and small gardens. There are seven typical reasons.

(1) The pleasure and stimulation of watching pet fish feed, swim by, grow and breed, and birds drinking from the pond.
(2) The added interest from visiting or resident frogs, toads, damsel and dragonflies as the pond matures. Normally this occurs within 18-24 months. It may be quicker depending on your location in relation to barrancos and lakes.
(3) The creation of a humid microclimate around the pond that can support more moisture living plants than in other areas in the garden. Constructing a marsh area alongside the pond can enhance the impact.
(4) The possibility of growing water lilies. A number of colours and types grow easily and are obtainable in coastal garden centres.
(5) The summer evening chorus of croaking frogs in addition to the sound of crickets. We enjoy this, but it may not be to everyone's liking.
(6) The impact on garden vistas of reflections on the surface of the pond water.
(7) The relaxing sound of water from a fountain or waterfall.

Naturally, there are also risks associated with installing a pond:
(1) The backbreaking effect of digging it out if unfit. Contract out the work if you have a bad back or heart.
(2) A pond can be a danger to resident and visiting young children. The pond therefore needs to be fenced off or covered with a strong wire mesh cover until the children are of a safe age. Naturally, the safety fence or cover can be permanent or temporary. Preferably the pond should be visible from the house but sited away from a main path. It is a good idea to surround most of the pond with a metre of rockery.
(3) If the pond is too shallow it can dry out quickly in the summer and become stagnant. Aim to have the central areas 60 to 100cm deep.
(4) The pond may also attract insects that breed in its microclimate. These may include gnats and mosquitoes. However, our experience of having several ponds on the Costa is that the fish and frogs speedily devour any hatching larvae.
(5) Ponds do attract drinking bees and wasps, but no more than flowers, fruit trees and a wet lawn.

How large should the pond be?
This is a personal decision. An elderly neighbour is very happy with one square metre, 30cm deep pond. The thriving residents include three goldfish, four frogs and a miniature water lily. The roots are constrained by planting on a small container without holes. This small pond is an attractive feature in a flowerbed alongside the terrace where they eat. One can also be created in a half wine barrel or large earthenware pot. If you have a sloping garden, perhaps an old barranco or series of terraces, it is possible to construct a series of small pools with waterfalls between them. The pools need only be a half to two square metres to sustain a collection of waterside plants with fish in the larger pools. The waterfalls can be operated by means of a circulating pump submerged in the lowest pool with a pipe feeding the top pool.

Alternatively the top pool can be fed by a trickling hose for an hour every few days to make up for any evaporated water. If this is done when you are having a siesta or meal by the pool you will have the sound of 'music' but without the expense of a pump.

Also one can build a larger pond or mini lake as a major feature. A 10 to 15 square metre pond will support several mature water lilies, banks of irises etc., and a shoal of sizeable fish.

What shape should the pool be?
If the garden is a rustic cottage-type garden, an irregular or oval pond would probably achieve the most pleasing effect. If your garden is, or will be, formal or modernistic in design, a more regular square, oblong or round pond would probably be most pleasing.

Where should the pond be sited?
Best in an open sunny or lightly shaded area. In full shade the pond water will tend to discolour with floating algae. Not a good condition for plants or fish. Don't worry about full sun; plants will soon give plenty of shade for the fish.

If your chosen site for the pond is rock-free up to a metre deep it is easy to dig out and line a pond with a flexible butyl lining or a preformed reinforced glass fibre pond. If using a butyl lining avoid joins if possible. In both cases the pond can be immediately filled with water that will eventually house plants and fish etc.

If your soil is rocky or stony it will be preferable to construct a reinforced concrete pond. The best pools have sloping, stepped sides. This provides a range of depths for various groups of aquatic and marginal plants.

44. Garden pond - stocking

Having constructed the pond it now needs to be stocked with plants and fish. But with what? There is a very wide choice..

The following guidelines are based on our experience with ponds in Mediterranean gardens.

1. Fill the newly constructed pond with water. If you use domestic water, add a proprietary chlorine neutraliser. Most aquarium shops will be able to advise you on what they stock and how to use.

2. Leave the pond for a week before starting to add plants in the margins and in deeper water.

A. Marginal Plants

The following five are suggested as a start:
- Yellow marsh irises or multicoloured Japanese irises.
- Pond mint
- Gunnera - large leaved, looking like rhubarb
- Marsh marigold, calla palustris and zantedeschia aethiopica
- Primula japonica

Plant in plastic or earthenware pots leaving plenty of room for root expansion. Before planting weight down the pots with five centimetres of concrete in a plastic bag in the base. Plant plants in a good compost mix. Cover the top of the soil with coarse sand or grit and firm down well.

Lower pots into the pond water placing them on the outer shallow ledge. Move plants round until the layout creates a pleasing effect. They will soon grow to provide weed cover, and a route for frogs to enter and leave.

B. Totally submerged plants

Oxygenating plants are essential to a healthy pond. The easiest to obtain are probably:
- The feathery myriophyllum verticillatum
- Elodea canadensis
- Potamogeton natans

Grow in pots or open plastic cages placed on the bottom of the pond. They should soon grow into natural looking weed beds.

C. Floating plants

These plants do not need to be planted in soil. Just place a cutting in the pond and it will grow to provide summer shade for the fish. Many also flower. Try the following:
- Eichhornia crassipes - bluey white flowers
- Hydrocharis morsus-ranae - white flowers
- Stratiotes aloides - white flowers

D. Emergent Plants

These plants need to be planted in weighted pots or baskets placed on the bottom or side shelves of the pond. The following have exotic flowers:
- Water lilies such as nymphaea caroliniana or marliacea
- Lotus flowers - nymphaea lotus
- Ludwigia clavellina
- Eriophorums

Don't over plant. Aquatic and margin plants tend to grow rapidly in the warm water conditions. Allow three or four weeks for the plants to settle roots and improve the water before starting to add fish. If possible obtain some water snails to keep the pond hygienic.

3. You are now ready to add fish.

Start by adding just a few. Check that they settle in quickly and don't appear to be stressed by the new pond conditions. Then add progressively.

A small half square metre pond can support three or four five-centimetre long fish. A large pond of say 15 square metres can probably support a shoal of 20 five-centimetre long fish, ten 10-centimetre long fish and five 25-centimetre long fish. Once the fish start to breed you will have shoals of fry and then young fish. They grow quickly. If you have too many fish their growth will be stunted and the largest fish may begin to starve and die. Check your stocking levels annually. Give away surplus small fish.

The above are basic guidelines. A pond with a fountain or waterfall and natural food in the mud will support more than a new, or regularly cleaned, sterile pool.

The best choice of fish are goldfish or koi carp. The variously coloured shabunkins and sturgeons look attractive in a pond but are less hardy in the winter.

Buy from an aquarium shop rather than the market. Check that there are no diseased fish in the stock tank that you are purchasing from.

Many shops pack the fish in a sealed plastic bag half full of water. Fish can normally survive for an hour or two in such conditions. But avoid a very hot day for buying them.

Float the container in the pond for half an hour to balance water temperatures before releasing the fish.

Few ponds will have enough natural food to sustain the health and growth of all the fishpond. Feed pond fish every other day in the summer and weekly in the winter. The safest food is a mix of proprietary fish food granules and flakes. A well-formulated food will also include the trace vitamins etc., necessary for healthy, good-coloured fish.

THE ONLY MAINTENANCE REQUIRED IS AS FOLLOWS:

a. Remove any dead fish as soon as seen.

b. If plants float up to the surface, especially water lilies, remove and re-pot, ensuring that the weight of the pot is sufficient to hold the plant on the bottom of the pond. Secure plants in the pot with copper wire.

c. Remove any dead plants. Cut back dead lily leaves and flowers to stimulate new growth and prevent the build up of rotting leaves.

d. In the autumn, using a net, remove tree or shrub leaves that blow into the pond.

e. If the pond goes green or becomes covered with algae treat with a proprietary solution available from an aquarium shop. You can also throw some straw in.

f. Top up the pond weekly to replace evaporated water.

g. If you live in a frost belt, float a plastic duck or ball on the pond to keep a clear area of water when ice forms.

h. Kingfishers do visit garden ponds. If you start to lose fish this way put a light net over the pond.

i. Every two or three years, split up large plants in the early spring when they show signs of growth.

We hope that you will enjoy a thriving pond for years to come.

45. Constructing a rockery

A rockery is an interesting and colourful feature in many Costa gardens, making use of natural resources - local rocks and drought resistant plants.

WHAT IS A ROCKERY?

For practical purposes a rockery is an area of a garden which is 60-80 per cent covered by rocks of various sizes with a variety of plants growing in the gaps between the rocks.

WHERE TO BUILD A ROCKERY?

In our view there are four best places to build a rockery. Best in that they take advantage of natural features.

A. A rocky slope, especially if you inherit an area of sloping bedrock or an area of natural hillside left uncovered by builders.
B. A Mozarabic rock wall and terrace above.
C. Around a pond, or the sloping bank around a raised or semi-raised swimming pool.
D. A pile of builder's rubble.

WHY BUILD A ROCKERY?

Our experience is as follows-
a. Little maintenance once built.
b. Colourful and interesting 12 months of the year.
c. Uses natural Mediterranean plants.
d. Requires little watering. .
e. A good way to use a pile of rocks already in the garden or on local rough ground.
f. Multi-level gardens add interest.
g. A good way of covering up a pile of builder's rubble.

HOW TO START

A. If you have a natural rock strewn slope
- Clear off any builders rubble.
- Clear and stack loose rocks in graded heaps.
- Clear out unsightly mature gorse. Possibly keep younger plants.
- Identify and trim natural herbs, shrubs, perennials, miniature palms, bulbs and oak trees that exist.
- Trim to remove any dead flowers and unsightly branches to create balanced shapes and to stimulate new growth.
- Small self-seeded oak trees and carobs can be trimmed back every six months to retain them as wild bonsais.
- Remove all grass and unwanted plants between the rocks.

B. If you have an old Mozarabic wall/terrace
- Clear out any weeds from between the rocks in the wall, in front of and above.

C. For above the wall or round a swimming pool or pond
- Collect or purchase a pile of rocks roughly 30cm to 60cm square. Be careful when moving rocks, especially the larger ones. Use help and lifting gear if necessary.

D. If your start point is a pile of rubble
- Shape the pile to create an aesthetic base for the rockery.
- Collect or purchase rocks and a load of topsoil.

CONSTRUCTING AND PLANTING THE ROCKERY

The best method is to integrate the moving and placing of rocks with the planting of the main plants. In this way the rocks can be used to cover the newly planted roots. This gives shelter and reduces water evaporation, thus keeping roots cool and damp. Very important in the summer months. Use a gritty well draining humus rich soil for planting. Plant plants in groups as a patchwork quilt for maximum impact.

A. On an existing hillside plant plants in every hole and crevice between rocks and infill with smaller rocks so that the area is eventually totally covered with rocks .

B/C. On a terrace wall infill all the large crevices with herbs and succulents and the smaller ones with natural drought resistant succulents. Above the wall and around a swimming pool or pond, rocks are best placed in groups of three or four. Decide on your basic layout. Dig holes large enough to bury a third of each rock. Place the rocks and settle in. Remove the front rock. Dig a hole and plant plants so that the roots will be 50 per cent shaded by the rock when replaced. Fill in the planting hole, firm and replace the rock. Mulch around the plants with small rocks and rock chippings. Continue to cover the whole area. Use rocks of various sizes and shapes and the natural lie of the land to create a natural hillside effect.

D. With a pile of rubble start by covering the pile with 10cm of soil. Water well to wash between the rocks. Repeat until all the rocks are covered. Add a final 25cm layer of soil. Then proceed as for B and C above.

PLANTING PLANTS

The inherited natural plants will soon spread to fill the holes between rocks. Concentrate therefore on planting in the spaces between rocks that have no natural plants.

Select from the following to create a rockery that suits your garden setting:- perennial herbs, especially rosemary, thyme, sage, rue and lavender - rock roses - brooms - succulents - cacti - dwarf lantanas, purple, yellow and white - gazanias - spring and summer bulbs - mesembryanthemums.

The above offer you a wide choice of shapes, colours and heights. We suggest that you plant small plants. They transplant and set down healthy roots quicker than a larger often root-bound plant.

The latter often die. They cannot obtain sufficient water even though a wild plant of the same size is drought resistant.

Plants from hillsides are often difficult to transplant. And it is illegal in many cases to remove them.

In the second and third year you will probably find that many self-seeded hillside plants appear. Select the most attractive, clear other as weeds. Once planted a rockery will require little expenditure if any on replacement plants. Most plants that thrive can be raised from seed or cuttings. They are best started in pots rather than putting them directly into the rockery.

WATERING

Water plants when first planted and through the first summer. Then stop watering from September to June to encourage plants to develop a deep root system. Water in the second and subsequent summers if there is no rain for a month. Plants will survive without, but a little water will encourage flowering. The exception are cacti they prefer less water. But spray.

WEED CONTROL

Remove grass and weeds from between rocks every couple of months, top up with mulch around plants to discourage further weeds. You can also plant plants on the rockery through black plastic and then cover the plastic sheeting with small rocks and grit.

If in doubt about a new plant that springs up leave it until it flowers. You can then decide to retain it or regard it as a weed to be removed. A natural hillside has an enormous diversity of natural plants.

FEEDING

None generally required.

The construction of a rockery will require a few days of hard labour. But the reward will be a part of the garden that improves year after year with little maintenance.

46. Review of garden furniture and ornaments

It is not only layouts and plants that make a garden, but also the aesthetics, choice and placing of garden furniture and ornaments. Very often we purchase a house in Spain and bring previous furniture and ornaments with us, inherit from previous owners or purchase something inexpensive to get us through the first summer. Often they clash, at least in time. Basic white plastic tables and chairs may look fine on a bare plot and on the pool terrace. But in time they do not blend in with the emergent ambiance and carefully cultured colour effects from flowers and leaves. Fortunately or unfortunately there are many designs to choose from, and each year new forms and materials appear on the market. We therefore suggest that you audit the situation in your garden every so often. The questionnaire on the left is designed to help you be objective and speed the process.

If you score entirely "definitely" we congratulate you. Don't change. Where you score partially, consider what you could do before replacing anything - which could be expensive. Consider changing seat covers or a repainting. Modern paints allow one to easily repaint plastic, metal or wood to the colour and tint of your choice. If you score numerous "noes" again consider whether 'do it yourself' changes could make the furniture acceptable before you do anything. When making new purchases consider what they will look like new and when weathered and worn. When you do look out for new furniture etc., you will see that the choice becomes bigger and bigger. Thus more confusing! In making choices it is important to remember that you are furnishing your garden, not that of the salesperson or persons accompanying you. Only you can decide what fits in with your vision of your garden and aesthetic taste. The latest fashion furniture may not fit in as well as a well-tested traditional design.

REVIEW QUESTIONNAIRE

Does the design, colour, fabric and texture of the following blend in with and enhance our planned or maturing garden?	REACTIONS		
	Definitely	Partially	No
A. GARDEN FURNITURE			
1. Tables and chairs			
2. Pool sun beds			
3. Other sun beds and deck chairs			
4. Sky chairs or hammocks			
5. Umbrellas or awnings			
6. Permanent or portable barbecue			
7. Oven			
8. Jacuzzi			
B GARDEN ORNAMENTS AND ARTIFACTS			
9. Garden pots and urns			
10. Window boxes			
11. Statues			
12. Other sculptures			
13. Bird bath			
14. Bird boxes			
15. Fountains			
16. Garden frame			
17. Greenhouse			
18. Compost heap			
19. Potting table			
20. Hose reels			

47. Christmas plants - purchasing

Every year many plants purchased for Christmas don't survive more that a few months and many newly presented tools don't leave the tool shed. Yet a little pre-thought could avoid many of the embarrassments.

First, the issue of plants.

Why do we continue to buy the houseplants that don't last, for relations and friends at Christmas? Plants such as azaleas, cyclamens, miniature roses, hydrangeas and poinsettias. They are often over forced in hot greenhouses to be out in full bloom during the Christmas week when the house is probably already full of colour from the Christmas tree, cards and decorations.

If the plants have been forced, they may be in a state of shock when handed over to the recipient. Within a matter of a few weeks or even days the plants may have left a greenhouse in Holland, been transported to Spain (hopefully in a climate-controlled container), delivered to the wholesaler, delivered to the garden centre or florist, taken home by yourself and then delivered to the recipient. For a tender plant the combination of frequent changes of temperature, moisture, humidity, draughts and light may be a major shock.

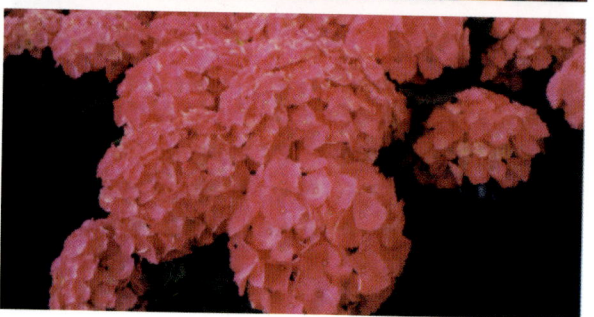

WHEN BUYING PLANTS AT CHRISTMAS WE SUGGEST THE FOLLOWING ACTION:

a. check with the garden centre the source of the plants and how long they have had them in stock. If the plants have or are coming into flower in the garden centre they are probably safer plants to buy than those delivered in full bloom that day by an overnight lorry.

b. check that parts of the plant, leaves or new flower buds are not starting to go yellow or die back, due to over or under watering or possible disease.

c. buy a plant that has one or two buds coming out so that you can check the colour but which has plenty of strong buds that will open up over the next weeks or in some cases months.

d. check that the soil in the pot is just damp. Beware of a dry or soaking wet pot. Check the condition of roots that may be showing through holes in the pot.

e. if you are buying an interesting plant that is new to you, ask the garden centre for instructions on how to best care for the plant i.e. watering top or bottom and how frequently; sunny or shady position; near or away from draughty doors; possibility of putting out on the terrace or even eventually planting out in the garden; and the possibility of taking cuttings to propagate new plants.

f. deliver the plant to the final recipient as soon as possible with the full instructions. Perhaps they would enjoy the flowering plant the week before Christmas more than over Christmas itself.

g. consider buying evergreen succulent plants or cacti. They are normally more hardy and can be enjoyed for years as they mature. A bowl of bulbs to flower in January could also give much pleasure. In fact why buy a plant for the house or naya? Why not buy a shrub or tree for the garden?

The local choice is enormous. But make sure that you purchase something that will fit into the emerging garden of the person(s) you are buying for. There are of course alternatives to plants. Carefully selected seeds, bulbs, tools, books, protective hand cream or subscriptions to gardening magazines are often unexpected and delightful gifts. There are a few households that would not appreciate another pair of secateurs or two pairs of gardening gloves - one glove always seems to disappear.

Happy Christmas Shopping!

48. Christmas plants - aftercare

We now look at how to handle plants that you receive for Christmas. The advice is designed to help you ensure that the plants settle into their new microclimate and survive.

At Christmas time many of us receive gifts of houseplants. Often we don't seem to have many 'green fingers'. Many of us have to admit that in Spain many poinsettias, azaleas, cyclamens, hydrangeas etc., die and don't make it to a second season and an eventual planting out in the garden.

There are probably a number of reasons for our problems. We are not helped by the following factors:

Imported Christmas flowering plants have often been forced at a high temperature and humidity and with 24 hours artificial light. This preparation is more suited to a transfer to a light, airy, constant temperature, centrally heated house or flat. Imported for sale in Spain they are often in a state of shock when transported, displayed in a cool garden centre and moved to a cool non-centrally heated villa at 25-20C, which rises 10 degrees when the stove in the living room is lit in the evening.

Rarely are there convenient internal windowsills or even large windows on the cooler west or north sides of the house. And the south facing windows, unless they open onto a naya, are hotter than a greenhouse.

THE CYCLAMEN

One of the most popular plants given as a gift is the cyclamen. A plant that bears a fantastic head of flowers for several months, year after year if well cared for. Remember that cyclamens grow on the edge of woodlands in the wild, in a damp sunny spot.

To reduce the initial shock you have hopefully been given a plant that is just coming into flower rather than being in full flower. This has the maximum chance of survival. It has probably been in a forcing house for only a short period of time or even better been grown in a cool greenhouse. Water only when the soil becomes dry and the plants just looks a little thirsty, water from the base but don't drown. Over watering will soon result in yellow leaves and the drooping and rotting off of unopened flower buds.

A rescued cyclamen in April

Try putting cyclamens on a table in the naya but out of the direct midday sun. One problem you face is that the fully flowering plant you have been given is in fact at the end of its flowering season and almost ready to hibernate naturally. Who knows at the time of purchase? If this appears to be the case try the following action. When the growth above the cyclamen corm seems to be withering away, take it out of the pot it is in and re-pot in a slightly larger clay pot. Keep the tuber at the same level as before relative to the soil level. Cut off any withered flowers and leaves. Put the plant in a cool corner and forget it. Water around the sides of the pot avoiding the tuber, every two weeks. After approximately two months new growth will start appearing. Put pot back into the light; commence watering regularly as the plant grows steadily to flowering size. Also one of the secrets to achieving strong plants that flower over a long period of time is to grow them under a special plant light.

THE POINSETTIA

The poinsettia is probably the second favourite Christmas plant. This also often survives longer if kept outside in the naya. If you do start off with a lovely healthy plant that then gradually loses all its leaves until you are left with a straggly plant don't give up and immediately throw it out. Try nursing it back to full glory for next Christmas and take cuttings. It is worth a try.

First cut back any spindly stems left to 15-20cm and put the plant in an out of sight corner. Continue to water but gradually cut back to a small cup per week as the plant become dormant. When you see new shoots appearing in the spring put the plant back into good light. Water and feed regularly. By late spring the plant should have strong new leaves and branches. These are your source of cuttings. Cut off each stem just before the third node. Plant in a sandy soil in a clay pot. Place the pots inside clear plastic bags. Blow the bags full of air and seal. These mini greenhouses will maintain the humidity required to root. After a month check gently to see if they are rooted. When strong roots are established lift out of the pot and re-pot in good potting soil in a larger pot. Poinsettias need very bright light to flower well. As with cyclamens a plant light helps. They also need 15 hours of darkness a day to match their natural African climate. So if you want flowers on your cuttings the following year, start planning in January. In mid November place the new plants in a cupboard (no light at all) at 17.00 until 08.00 next day. Perhaps for most of us it is easier to buy or receive a new plant each Christmas!

THE AZALEA

Another popular Christmas plant. Again it needs plenty of light. If your house is light, keep it inside over Christmas for its flower display. Put outside when flowering is finished. Otherwise put on the north side of the house preferably in a sheltered porch with plenty of light. Avoid direct sunlight all day long. As it grows bigger, re-pot. Feed regularly while in flower.

THE CHRISTMAS CACTI

The Christmas cacti are lovely plants to receive for Christmas. Again don't over water, as they like to be on the dry side. This plant comes in many colours. It is easy to take cuttings. Plant them in a plant mix of soil and sand. The cuttings are similar to the poinsettia. They need a long dark night in the autumn to stimulate flowers for Christmas.

As a general rule remember that indoor flowering plants like a bright position but not direct sunlight. Also that just under watering is better than over watering. Keep out of draughts and frequently changing temperatures.

If you receive hard leafed non flowering plants such as a rubber plant, aspidistra, mother-in-law's tongue, or a fern, these are more suitable for cool, shady places than flowering plants. They survive well in the house and on the naya. Likewise pots of bulbs are happy and flower longer in a cool spot.

49. *The vegetable garden in February/March*

There is nothing to beat daily picked or freshly dug vegetables throughout the year, but it does need dedication, time and perseverance. Especially if you grow organically.

The local seasons, climate and therefore vegetable planting cycles are very different to northern Europe.

If you have yet to start growing vegetables, you have three choices - don't, start now or wait till the autumn.

STARTING FROM SCRATCH NOW

February and March are good months to start. Provided you have an inexpensive and reliable supply of agricultural water from a village irrigation system or a well. If you don't, delay your start till the autumn and only grow winter crops. The essential first jobs: -

a. Clear the land of all weeds, especially perennial weeds and burn.

b. Plough the land or double dig if only a small plot.

c. Ten days later, provided it has not rained, harrow the land by rotavator or hand harrow. Unfortunately we had to wait four weeks for the right soil conditions.

You are now ready to join the annual cycle followed by gardeners who already have an established vegetable garden.

PREPARATION FOR AN AUTUMN START

If you decide to wait till the autumn, cover your selected plot with a layer of compost and/or well-rotted manure and cover with newspapers and a sheet of black plastic until September. Worms will work the organic material into the soil during the summer and weeds will not grow. Also start a compost heap. Incorporate the household vegetable waste, soft garden cuttings and grass cuttings.

ANNUAL JOBS FOR MARCH/APRIL

1. Plant a last sowing of broad beans. Late sowings run the risk of black fly infestation when the weather warms up. Pinch out the tops when the first pods form. This removes the favourite habitat for black flies.

2. Spray autumn sowings of broad beans against black fly with a soap spray or a proprietary spray if you have not changed over to organic principles.

3. Stake up winter peas, which should now be well up and probably flowering.

4. Plant early potatoes. Put the seed potatoes in a dark warm place for a week or two to stimulate sprouting before planting. Get your potatoes off to a good start by under laying them with a layer of rotted compost or manure and a five-centimetre layer of comfrey leaves if available.

5. Complete the winter cleanup. Compost annual weeds but stack and burn rye grass roots and perennial plants. Obtain a licence and have the bonfire on a non-windy day. Have a supply of water handy in case the fire starts to get out of control.

6. Remove yellow leaves from brassicas and spray against white fly weekly. Sprays of washing up liquid, and crushed garlic can be effective. Continue to be vigilant until the last Brussels sprouts, broccoli, cauliflowers and cabbages are eaten. Compost the removed leaves unless seriously diseased.

7. Watch for carrot fly on carrots planted in the autumn. Make a companion planting of onions or use a garlic infusion.

8. Plant main crop onion seedlings and feed monthly with a comfrey, nettle or diluted manure solution.

9. Rake over the asparagus bed and top up with ten centimetres of soil and five centimetres of well-rotted manure. Most raised beds settle each year. The deeper soil will help to blanch emergent asparagus tips in the spring.

10. Prepare beds for spring sowing. If you have them, cover with old carpets or black plastic to prevent weed growth and help warm up the beds prior to planting in April and May.

11. Plant up a selection of vegetables in tubes, pots or seed boxes and place in a cold frame or under a plastic sheet for protection. Water weekly to keep the soil damp but not wet. Vegetables that can be started early include the following: - spring onions, lettuces, radishes, tomatoes (+), cucumbers (+), peppers (+), aubergines (+) squashes (+) and pumpkins (+). The (+) indicates that these vegetables are best started by growing plantlets in tubes or pots filled with potting compost. There is no need to purchase potting trays. The cores of toilet rolls and kitchen paper work well but few will be available. A quick inexpensive solution is to prepare newspaper tubes. Our experience is that climbing beans and melons are best left until April.

12. Prepare frames for climbing beans ready for planting seeds or plantlets in April. Ensure that the canes are tied firmly together and the end posts well secured.

13. Plant out final strawberry plantlets. Make a large cloche or frame to cover them.

14. If not done already cut back old raspberry canes and repair posts and wires ready for tying in new canes in the spring. Deep mulch with grass cuttings and well-rotted manure. Do likewise with cultivated blackberries and loganberries.

15. Collect seaweed from the beach after a storm. Give the asparagus bed a covering. Wash the remainder to remove salt and stack to dry for a few weeks. Then add to manure and mulches during the spring to enhance the trace element content.

50. *The vegetable garden in April/May*

April and May are always very busy months before the hot growing and early ripening months of June and July.

Potatoes planted early February are already showing leaf; onions are making good progress, as are the carrots planted before Christmas. Broad beans and peas have been picked for some weeks and many of the over-wintered cauliflowers and cabbages have been eaten. Now is the time to make sowings for summer crops and care for earlier sowings and perennials.

The most important tasks are as follows:

1. Asparagus spears are now growing strongly, but unless your plants are three years old, resist the temptation to cut. If not done earlier, collect some seaweed from the shore and scatter between plants.

2. Potatoes are now sprouting through the soil. Earth them up further to achieve greater crops.

3. As winter brassicas finish, clear the plot and prepare beds for follow on crops of squash and melons. Fork in plenty of well-rotted manure.

4. During May plant out the squash, pumpkin and courgette plants raised from March sowing in pots. Initially cover with a cloche or clear plastic sheet until cold winds have finished.

5. Melons can be started in pots in April or wait to plant seeds direct in the second half of May. Cucumbers can be similarly sown.

6. Make early sowings of climbing and dwarf beans. Follow on with successive sowing fortnightly.

7. Lettuce plantlets can now be planted out together with strong tomato plantlets. Sow further lettuces and radishes directly into seedbeds. Cover a few tomato plants with a frame covered in clear plastic sheet to achieve early crops. Alternatively cut the base out of a five litre plastic water bottle and put over each plant; secure by putting a stick through the top down into the soil. You have probably been picking peas for some weeks. Follow on crops of pod peas or mangetout can still be planted.

8. Similarly, second main crop sowings of carrot and parsnip can be made. If you are worried about carrot fly, surround them with a 50cm high fence of plastic mesh. Normally carrot fly cannot fly that high. Also plant late onions or leek plantlets on the outside of carrot rows. If possible plant the carrots in a north south direction. Crops can then be stimulated by surrounding the carrots and onions with a thin copper wire supported on canes and earthed. This is said to reinforce the impact of the earths magnetic field.

9. Any beetroot plantlets grown in seed boxes or pots can be safely planted out in April. Also make direct sowings on the plot.

10. Plant some interesting and tasty salad vegetables from seed. Try rocket, purslane and new varieties of radish

11. April is a good time for a first planting of pepper and aubergine plantlets. Make a second planting during May.

12. Sweet corn and sunflowers make good windbreaks. They do well as companion plants.

13. Herbs such as parsley, chives, coriander, dill and fennel can be planted now. They grow well amongst vegetable crops. Coriander, fennel and dill have the benefit of attracting beetles from other plants. They can be easily picked off.

14. Be on the lookout for early infestations especially if spring showers and sun result in high humidity conditions.

15. Inspect the potato plants at least weekly. Pick off and destroy beetles, usually found on the underside of the leaves Wipe off any clumps of yellow eggs with tissue paper and then burn.

16. Artichokes are often infested with aphids in the early spring. Wash off as many as you can with a small brush and soapy water. Follow up with sprays of garlic or horsetail infusion.

17. If snails become a nuisance, especially around lettuces, strawberries, squash and melon plants, try some alternatives to the traditional snail pellets. The latter being dangerous to birds and reptiles.

The following ecological solutions work for us.

- Pick up and destroy snails as they appear.
- Surround young plants with a circle of comfrey leaves or prickly oak leaves
- Set up beer traps, sunk into the earth at strategic locations.
- Place damp cardboard held down with a stone at strategic locations around the plot; turn the cardboard over every few days, pick off and destroy the snails that assemble.

18. As the weather heats up, water all vegetables and plants regularly to stimulate continuous growth.

19. Vegetables make good growth during May but so do unwanted weeds. Weed or hoe beds regularly. Add them to the compost heap. Don't let weeds go to seed.

20. Feed young vegetable plants regularly. As organic/ecological enthusiasts, we feed with a liquid feed made up from well-rotted manure with a comfrey liquid supplement. The latter helps plants to extract important trace elements from the soil. See Chapter 76 for more details.

21. When squash, pumpkins and melon plants start to grow fast, pick out the growing tips to achieve compact, strong plants. Remove excess young fruit to achieve larger specimens.

As we said at the beginning, April and May will be busy months. The effort will hopefully be rewarded with fresh tasty salads and vegetables throughout the summer and early autumn.

51. *The vegetable garden in June/July*

The vegetable plot is now almost fully planted. Plants are growing fast. Early crops such as asparagus, peas, broad beans, carrots, lettuces and early potatoes have already been enjoyed. June and July are essentially months of weeding, watering, feeding and pest control. And of course planting seeds for later crops to be planted out in the autumn. We discuss each of these in turn.

1. WEEDING

Weeds are a problem. They smother young vegetable plants, suck up valuable water and minerals and of course look unsightly. The most effective means of weed control are as follows -

- Hand weeding - time consuming but foolproof.
- Hoeing - but you may distribute new seeds and you leave most of the roots in the ground.
- Planting plants through black plastic or old carpets.
- Close planting to smother weeds.
- Mulching around plants especially tomatoes and peppers that like to be continuously fed.
- Scorching with a butane weed wand
- As a last resort some people use weed killers. We do not recommend this, as we are organic gardeners. It can affect nearby vegetables and kill off beneficial insects and microbes in the soil. Long term a very sterile soil will result.

Weeds can be safely put on the compost heap during the summer. But keep the heap damp and mix in some manure or compost as an accelerator. Comfrey and dandelion leaves are also very good accelerators.

2. WATERING

This is the main watering period during the year. We flood our vegetable garden every seven to ten days. The timing depending on the temperatures and whether it has rained. Young plants need watering by hand in between to ensure that growth is not inhibited.

If you are not on an old irrigation system, water your vegetables via a hose or a drip system. Or perhaps a good idea would be to copy the old Moorish irrigation system and flood your small plot as we do.

Recognise, especially with a watering system, that a thorough deep soaking every week is better than a light daily wash. It is the deep roots that need the moisture.

3. FEEDING

The practice of crop rotation will ensure that seeds and plantlets are planted in appropriately preconditioned soil.

The most appropriate sequencing of crops on the Costas is as follows over a two year period.

GROUP	TYPICAL VEGETABLES
1	Potatoes - early/late
2	Root crops - carrots, parsnips, radishes
3	Onions - leeks, onions, garlic
4	Fruits - peppers, tomatoes, aubergines
5	Legumes - peas, beans
6	Brassicas - cauliflowers, broccoli
7	Squashes - courgettes, pumpkins, melons

- Heavy pre-manuring is essential for good crops of squashes and potatoes.
- Avoid adding fresh manure for root crops, as they will develop deformed/multi roots.
- Mulch fruits with well-rotted manure.
- Dig a trench and line with newspaper and well-rotted manure before planting legumes
- Brassicas may require that the soil is pre-treated with lime.
- During the summer feed plants weekly with a dilute solution made from well-rotted nettles and comfrey. These will help activate the extraction of growth stimulating minerals from the soil.
- For prize leeks, tomatoes, pumpkins try an additional feed of dilute liquid manure - made by putting well-rotted sheep/horse manure in a barrel with water and leaving for several weeks. We prefer the above organic feeds. Naturally organic granular chemicals can be used but their long term cumulative benefits are likely to be less.

4. PEST CONTROL

Pest control is covered in Chapter 55.

5. SUMMER PLANTINGS

Three types of planting can be made during June and July.

a. Follow on seed crops for continuity

During June plant some last lettuces, dwarf beans, carrots and radishes. These will provide produce through to the autumn.

b. Follow on plantlets for continuity.

We plant some late tomatoes and peppers, also melon plantlets, especially cantaloupe varieties. We pick our last tomatoes in February some years.

c. Grow plantlets for the autumn.

June/July is a good time to plant the following seeds for planting out in the autumn.

- Onions and leeks.
- Cabbage, cauliflower, brussels sprouts, broccoli, spinach etc. We find it more successful to plant the seeds in boxes rather than directly into the plot.

Place the boxes in large plastic bags, seal and keep in a shaded place to avoid scorching by the hot summer sun. This approach will keep emergent plants moist without the need for daily watering.

52. *The vegetable garden in August/September*

There is more to do during August and September than in the flower garden at this time of the year. But the benefit is continuing to eat fresh vegetables and salads daily. The following 13 tasks are considered the most important. They are based on our practical experience of working a vegetable garden in Spain and harvesting 365 days a year.

1. Watering - Watering has to be the number one priority through to mid-September. If your vegetable plot is connected to an agricultural water system, continue to flood every eight to 10 days. Naturally extending the time when storms occur. If you water by hose, water heavily every three or four days, or more lightly every evening if your plot is small. Recognise that vegetables such as lettuce and tomatoes will require most water and drying onions and melons the least.

2. Feeding - Better vegetables will be obtained by regular feeding. Useful feeds are solutions made up from water and compost, well-rotted manure, seaweed, nettles or comfrey leaves. Comfrey helps plants extract essential trace elements from the soil. If you use granular chemical fertilisers, dissolve them to reduce the chance of burning foliage and roots.

3. Combating Bugs - Inevitably a variety of bugs - beetles and aphids - will still appear during late summer.. Constant vigilance is required. Spray when they first appear and then every few days. We discuss sprays in a separate chapter on plant protection.

4. Weeding - A weekly hoe will keep most weeds under control. However, pull or dig out the strong perennial weeds before they seed. Proprietary butane weed burners are also becoming available in Spain. Used carefully they don't damage growing vegetables. But recognise the fire risk. Chemical weed killing is not a good idea during the growing season under any circumstances and in many areas is officially banned for fear of contaminating ground water and water flowing to adjacent plots.

5. Drying/Storing Vegetables - Ripe onions, melons, squash and potatoes should be dried for a few days before storing in a dark airy garage or dry cellar. Onions need to be dried for longer and they can then be strung up or hung up in open weave sacks. Melons, marrows and squashes can be stored on the floor in well-ventilated boxes or on strong shelves. Potatoes can be sacked, put in boxes or left in the ground until required. Carrots and beetroot can be stored in boxes in dry sand, peat or sawdust or as with potatoes left in the ground. All should keep beyond Christmas and the New Year. To protect your stored vegetables against infestations, hang up a sock or two of sodium metabisulphite in the storeroom.

6. Processing surplus crops - Naturally surplus crops of beans can be frozen. Vegetables such as tomatoes, courgettes, aubergines and peppers are better picked and made into a variety of chutneys or pesto for autumn or winter use.

SUGGESTED SEPTEMBER PLANTINGS TO PRODUCE CROPS FOR CHRISTMAS ARE:

Lettuce, endives and chicory for appetising multicoloured salads.

A row or two of potatoes. If above the frost level, protect with straw in November.

Spinach. Plant now and you can start to pick in November through to next April.

Onion seeds sown in September will produce salad onions for Xmas and seedlings for planting out in December to February for early full sized onions in the spring.

7. Winter tomatoes - Leave some of your favourite tomato plants in the ground. If we have a warm dry autumn they will continue to produce a few flowers and welcome late salad tomatoes.

8. Cleaning finished crops - Pull or dig out finished crops as soon as the last beans, potatoes, etc., have been picked. Put all undiseased stems, leaves and roots on the compost heap. Seal others in a plastic bag and put in the appropriate rubbish bin.

9. Preparing a new seed bed - Hoe or lightly dig the used beds. Cover with five centimetres of well-rotted compost or manure. And then cover the bed with a sheet of heavy cardboard or a piece of old carpet. This will prevent weed growth, retain moisture to attract worms that take the compost into the soil and keep the soil in a friable condition ready for raking just prior to planting new seeds. Leave the prepared beds two to eight weeks before making autumn sowings.

10. Preparing a vegetable plot for the first time - If you are only going to plant vegetables for the autumn, winter and early spring you will need to start to prepare your ground in early September. We suggest as follows:-

a. Clear the area of all existing growth especially deep-rooted perennial weeds. Have the area ploughed or rotavated.

b. Leave for two weeks.

c. Rotavate to a fine tilth.

d. Start to prepare seed beds for planting. If you decide to grow ecologically/organically, this is the last ploughing/rotavating you will need to do.

11. Audit the last year's successes and failures - August is an ideal time to reflect on the successes and failures of the last years' crops before planning for the next cycle of autumn, winter and spring sowings (see chapter 58).

12. Preplanning the sowings. - After the review prepare a planting chart for the next 12 months ensuring that appropriate crops are rotated to keep the soil in good condition and take advantage of the soil conditioning of the last crops. Follow this up with the early ordering of seeds to ensure that you obtain your first choice especially if ordering organically prepared seeds.

13. First autumn sowings - One of the delights of living on the Costa is the practicality of growing vegetables all year round except in the higher inland valleys we rarely experience low temperatures, frosts and icy winds. Planting can start in September. Autumn plantings can be divided into two groups.

a. Planting to produce crops for Christmas eating.

b. Plantings to produce crops for the late winter/early spring.

53. *The vegetable garden in October/November*

October and November are busy months in the vegetable garden, as on the Costa it is possible to raise many crops over the winter. The main tasks for the two months are as follows.

1. PREPARATION OF NEW PLOT

If you started to prepare your plot in the spring as described in Chapter 49, now is the time to complete the preparation. These are four ways as illustrated

- First remove any weeds growing on the plot. Burn the perennials and compost the annuals.
- Remove the plastic or carpet covers. You should find that the manure has disappeared. Well rotted and taken into the soil by worms. Also there will be few weeds under the plastic. Remove what are there.
- There should be no need to dig, only to break up the top 10cm with a harrow or large rake to develop a fine tilth for your first sowings.
- If you did not start preparations during the summer clear the plot of weeds, plough and harrow as soon as possible. Try to borrow a rotavator or even the village mule! The last resort is a manual double digging and raking.

2. COMPLETION OF AUTUMN SOWINGS

A. FOR CHRISTMAS CROPS
- If not already done plant a few lettuce plants.
- Sow seeds of endives, chicory, radishes rocket and some more lettuce for appetising multicoloured salads.
- If not done in September plant a row or two of potatoes. Cover part of the row with plastic making holes above the planted potatoes. This may help to force the potatoes for Christmas.

B. FOR WINTER/SPRING CROPS
- Plant out further purchased or self-grown brassica plants.
- Plant onion seedlings in both October and November also leeks.
- Plant sowings of broad beans each fortnight from the end of October to provide cropping over an extended period from February to May.
- Plant spinach.
- Peas planted during October and November will be ready to pick in February/March. We find that smooth seeded varieties stand up to the winter cold better than the wrinkled varieties. The latter withstand the heat better so sow these in February/March for picking in May/June. Check your lunar calendar for the best sowing dates.

3. WATERING

- Water in plantlets and seeds immediately after planting. Don't allow them to dry out in the first few weeks of planting. Especially important for the germination of seeds.
- You will probably not need to water further unless we have an exceptionally hot period, or don't have any autumn rain.

4. FEEDING

- Continue to feed fortnightly as recommended for September.
- We find that the most beneficial natural feeds are liquids made up from manure, comfrey and nettles. If you don't have any of the above there is a wide choice of liquid feeds available in the shops, either chemical or ecological.

5. THE AUTUMN CLEAN UP

- Clear away any end of summer/early autumn crops that have fruited. Compost if disease free.
- Leave a few strong tomato plants that show signs of continuing to flower rather than dying back. Feed fortnightly with liquid comfrey or a special tomato feed. With luck you will pick a few tomatoes through to January/February.

6. PREPARING SPRING SEED BEDS

- After your autumn planting and clean up, you will have areas of the vegetable plot that will not be planted up until the spring. Rather than allow new weeds to grow, cover these areas with two to four centimetres of manure or compost, and then cover with heavy plastic sheeting or old carpets. During the winter the organic material will rot down and be taken into the soil by an expanding population of worms. By spring you will have enriched soil that will require little working before planting up. This method also keeps the soil moist and warm. Look at your companion planting plan to decide on which areas to manure lightly and those to manure most heavily.

7. WEEDING

- As above. Cover up annual weeds to rot and recycle nutrients.

8. CHECK STORED CROPS

- Check through stored squashes, onions, potatoes, carrots, melons, etc. Use any that are going soft immediately and remove any that are rotting to the compost heap.

54. *The vegetable garden in December/January*

From our experience the following are the top 21 jobs to be carried out in December and January.

1. Stake up broad beans planted in September and October if they are becoming windblown because of their height. We hope to pick a few pods for Christmas Day from plants that flowered in mid-October.

2. Plant out some more broad bean seeds in December and January, by the lunar calendar. Also one or two rows of peas in a sheltered, warm garden.

3. Buy a lunar gardening calendar. The best we have discovered is published by Artus Porta, Calle Semes 58, E-43392 Castellvell del Camp. This should be available by ordering through a major bookshop. It is also stocked by some health shops and El Corte Inglés. It would make a good Christmas present.

4. Buy a bunch or two of onion plants. They are normally sold 100 or 200 a bunch. Plant these out eight to ten centimetres apart. You could also plant onion sets and garlic.

5. Earth up autumn planted potatoes. Hopefully you will have at least a small crop for Christmas.

6. Following the seasonal damp weather watch out for snails that are wandering out from the orange groves. Remove them by hand picking. If kept in a cage and fed with rosemary there is still time to prepare them for a New Year's tapas!

7. Pick lettuces regularly while young to avoid a later glut of fully mature plants about to go to seed.

8. Trim off any dead leaves of brassicas. Remove side leaves off Brussels sprouts to encourage sprouts to swell.

9. Earth up leeks to encourage thick stems.

10. Start some more leeks from seeds in seed boxes in a sunny frame.

11. Take herb cuttings of sage, rosemary, thyme, etc.

12. Divide beds of comfrey and nettles being grown for organic feeds.

13. Sow borage and other herbs in warm areas.

14. Watch carrots planted in the autumn for carrot fly if we have a hot spell.

15. Cut out old canes from raspberry bushes. Tie young canes to wires strung between strong posts. Do likewise with blackberries and loganberries.

16. Spray fruit trees and soft fruit bushes with a winter wash.

17. Add a manure mulch around soft fruit bushes.

18. Clean up unplanted areas of the vegetable plot of clumps of grass, old plants and weeds. Turn the compost heap and incorporate the new material.

19. Burn any perennial weeds with seed heads and diseased plants, especially tomato and pepper plants.

20. Prepare beds ready for planting potatoes, squashes, etc., in the spring. Double dig and incorporate plenty of well-rotted manure. Cover with cardboard, plastic or old carpets to stop weeds from growing.

21. If you have access to a plantation of canes, then cut canes for use next spring at the full moon in January. Local village folklore and our new lunar calendar both suggested this to ensure strong canes. Our past experience doesn't disagree.

55. Plant protection in the vegetable garden

Plant protection on the vegetable plot is a vital activity if good crops are to be harvested. The hot summer weather on the Costa, especially if humid, also breeds the natural enemies of the vegetable garden.

The main enemies are birds, bugs, aphids, fungi, snails and invading animals. We consider each in turn. Ecological solutions are offered where practical.

1. BIRD CONTROL

a. Construct one or two traditional scarecrows. Tie something that blows around in the wind to the ends of the arms to make the scarecrows look alive. Static arms provide convenient roosts for birds to select the best crop to attack! !
b. Tie a zigzag mesh of fishing line between 50cm posts. Tie on strips of aluminium foil.
c. Place a plastic net over plants such as peas and strawberries.
d. If all fails organise an occasional noisy Spanish 'mascleta'!

2. BUG CONTROL

a. Companion plants in strategically placed lines or patches e.g.
- Herbs such as dill, coriander and fennel. We find that various beetles are attracted preferentially in great numbers from other crops. Pick off or spray with natural insecticide.
- Roses, nasturtiums, marigolds, borage and zinnias. Ladybirds cleared any greenfly off the roses.

We found that within two years of planting the above our problem with bugs was minimal.
b. Spray beetles with a crushed garlic solution or a natural proprietary insecticide such as neem.
c. Do not kill off ants' nests. Ants love to feast on aphids.
d. A good winter and spring wash for fruit trees is an infusion of dried horsetail and nettle juice. Add some pigeon droppings if you can obtain them, the mix will be even more potent. You can also use a natural oil spray.
e. Pick off beetles and caterpillars and squash them.
f. If there is an angler in the family, keep any large maggots for fishing bait!
g. Plant any of the cabbage family near a row of tomatoes. Cabbage white butterflies do not like being near tomatoes. Also rub off any caterpillar eggs you see and pick off any caterpillars. Again you can spray with a natural insecticide.
h. If leaf curl appears on fruit trees immediately spray with the horsetail infusion as above.

3. APHID CONTROL

a. Spray susceptible plants with a dilute solution of natural potassium soap or a biologically degradable washing up liquid. Always use with unchlorinated water. A good natural insecticide is neem (extract from the nim tree).
b. Pick out the tips of broad beans after the first pods have formed, a favourite haven for black fly. If not already infested, steam the tips as an unusual vegetable.
c. String strips of aluminium foil on a fishing line above broad beans. Blackfly are apparently put off by the glitter!
d. Try placing yellow bottles among brassicas. The bottles attract the whitefly from the plants. Pour some bright yellow paint inside a few one-litre water bottles. Swill the paint around to coat the inside. When dry, fill the bottles with water to weight them. Place among the plants.
e. Plant nasturtiums near vegetables. They attract white and blackfly away from the vegetables. Pick and destroy seriously affected leaves and flowers.
f. Carrot fly - one weakness of the carrot fly is that they cannot fly high. So to protect your crop, put a mesh fence 45-50cm high around your crop, but it must be completely fly proof. Another solution is to plant onions among carrots to deter the smell. Don't plant carrots too densely to avoid thinning. You could also put a layer of seaweed around the plants.
g. Garlic infusions can also be used but preferably not or only as a last resort on artichokes, asparagus, aubergines, beans, cabbages and peas. If you do the effect will be the same as the negative companion planting effect from nearby garlic plants. If you have roses on your plot plant garlic cloves alongside and they will deter aphids.

4. FUNGI CONTROL

a. Spray the ground in which potatoes are sown with an infusion of horsetail to prevent mildew.
b. Dust with sulphur powder plants such as squashes, melons, courgettes, cucumbers, vines and tomatoes - sulphur rather than copper sulphate is organically acceptable, but use as little as possible. A good idea is to put some in a sock and shake over plants in the early morning when it is cool and normally little wind. Vines should be treated in the winter as well as summer. Wear goggles to protect your eyes.
c. Spray plants that are likely to be affected by mildew regularly with a horsetail infusion.
d. Remove affected leaves and destroy.

5. SNAILS

a. Place a square of damp corrugated cardboard at strategic points. Weigh them down with stones. Turn over and remove attracted snails every few days in the early morning or late evening.
b. Place a circle of comfrey leaves around young plantlets such as courgettes, melons and squashes and around fruiting strawberry plants.
c. Place a circle of prickly oak leaves threaded on fishing line around melon plants, lettuce seedlings etc.
d. Stick canes in the ground near vulnerable plants. Snails, especially smaller ones climb and stick to the cane. They are probably drinking the water droplets that condense on the canes overnight.
e. Sink plastic beakers filled with beer into the ground. Remove and destroy drunken snails every few days!

6. INVADING ANIMALS

a. Erect a strong post and wire fence.
b. Erect an electric fence.
c. If you have a rabbit warren nearby erect a wire mesh fence a metre high with 25cm of mesh buried in the soil.
d. Prickly pear cacti hedges were used in the past. One sometimes sees them on the outskirts of villages up to three metres high.

56. Comfrey - an invaluable herb

Comfrey, or consuelda in Spanish, is invaluable in the Spanish garden. Comfrey is a perennial herb. It is a member of the borage family that grows throughout Europe, both in gardens and in the wild. The plant has important medicinal and gardening properties. We suggest that you look out for a few plants to grow in a corner of the vegetable or flower garden.

MEDICINALLY

Poultices of the leaves and roots have been used for centuries to help heal injured tendons and fractured bones. Symphytum the generic name of comfrey comes from the Greek word "to unite". Comfrey extracts are apparently often an active ingredient in cosmetics and bath oils to regenerate aging skins.

HORTICULTURALLY/AGRICULTURALLY

Comfrey leaves are rich in potassium containing three times as much as farmyard manure. They also contain significant amounts of nitrogen, phosphorous and other minerals and therefore an excellent organic fertiliser in both the flower and vegetable garden. The leaves can be used in a number of ways:
a) by digging into the ground.
b) by laying under potatoes when sowing.
c) as a mulch. Used this way they are also an excellent, natural snail and slug repellent.
d) as a concentrated liquid feed.
e) added to the compost heap in layers to accelerate the rotting process and add nutrients.

THE PLANTS TO OBTAIN

There are several types of comfrey but look out for the Russian comfrey (type Bocking 14 organic). This has larger leaves and a higher concentration of nutrients than the common variety. The plant can grow to 1.5 metres in a damp fertile soil. It will flower in the summer but less profusely than the common comfrey. It will attract pollinators but is unlikely to self-seed. Russian comfrey is normally propagated by splitting up large plants in the autumn. A member of the borage family with rough, hairy, stemmed leaves and blue flowers that grow in droopy clusters throughout the summer.

ESTABLISHING A COMFREY BED

1. Obtain a few clumps of the Russian comfrey in the autumn or spring. They die back in winter and re-sprout in April.
2. Comfrey thrives in a rich moist soil. Select a good patch of soil where water collects when it rains. Dig it over and incorporate plenty of well-rotted manure or compost.
3. Split up the comfrey clumps into as many plantlets as possible. Plant them out 30cm apart and mark each with a stick. They will probably join up within two years.
4. Keep moist throughout the summer.
5. Pick leaves to use as soon as the plants are growing strongly, breaking stems off at the base. You will find that you can almost strip each plant three or four times a year.
6. You will find that the remaining leaves die off in November. The plants will probably re-sprout at the end of March/early April.
7. When they are dormant, lift mature plants and split.

PREPARING A LIQUID MANURE

We prepare a liquid manure in two ways. Both are easy.
1. Obtain a 20 to 30-litre plastic drum (not clear plastic), preferably with a low-level tap. Put the picked leaves into the drum and press down. Add two litres of water to help the decomposition process start. Cover the drum. Leave the leaves to decompose for two to four weeks.
2. Alternatively make a one-inch hole in the base of the drum. Raise the drum up on two bricks and place a container under the hole. Stuff the drum full of leaves but don't add any water and leave for four to six weeks. Gradually, liquid comfrey will drip into the container. By both methods you will now have a lovely, smelly, dark brown liquid. This is now ready to dilute for use.

USING LIQUID COMFREY

1. Liquid comfrey helps build strong plants. Strong plants resist disease.
2. Add one or two eggcups to five litres of water (the second method will be stronger, so add less).
3. Then feed to plants using a watering can.
4. All plants, flowers and vegetables will benefit. We find it especially beneficial to potatoes, leaf vegetables such as spinach and lettuce and to fruit vegetables such as tomatoes, peppers, aubergines, squashes and pumpkins. It helped us produce a 60-kilo entirely organic pumpkin.
5. A comfrey liquid feed is also excellent for pot plants as well as garden shrubs that need a boost.

MULCHING LARGE PLANTS

If you have plenty of leaves, use them to mulch around mature plants. They will probably provide shade for roots and help retain moisture. Gradually they rot down and provide a direct feed of liquid comfrey over a few months. Tomatoes, peppers, cauliflowers, melons and raspberries will all benefit from this treatment.

If you have trouble tracing Russian Comfrey plants, we know they are available by mail order from the following addresses. We suggest you first write for their catalogue.
Agroforestry Research Trust, 46 Hunters Moon, Darlington, Totnes, Devon TQ9 6JT and *Ragman's Lane Farm, Lower Lydbrook, Glos. GL17 9PA UK.*

57. Organic gardening - definitions and benefits

We look at organic gardening from the point of view of the small-scale domestic gardener, not the large-scale specialist farmer.

As a background, we assume that most expatriate residents came to Spain for a more active, more healthy, more satisfying and lower cost lifestyle. We, amongst many, assumed that this would include easier access than in northern Europe to a wide variety of freshly picked, tasty, crisp, good texture, long-keeping fruit and vegetables. Ten years ago, we found this. But gradually, at first stealthily and recently openly many supermarkets have removed free choice counters, reduced the range, dictated the size and ripeness of fruit and vegetables we can purchase by standardised plastic packaging of often unripe produce.

Luckily, we bought much of our vegetables and soft fruit in the open markets and village stores. The latter often supplied with daily fresh produce on a barter system. Even these traditional suppliers are dying or retiring. The younger generation is giving up or transforming to mass production farming methods, albeit on a small scale, of intensive artificial feeding, fumigation and plastic. For many the choice of traditional fresh produce is diminishing - and is likely to continue.

Against this background, we started a vegetable plot a few years ago. We wanted fresh, safe vegetables 365 days a year. We chose an organic, natural and ecological approach as it made sense and has proved to be fun. We are not organic addicts or activists. Just normal people concerned with getting the best from living in Spain and avoiding the hazards associated with the industrialisation of farms and food distribution. But first, what is organic or natural gardening for the amateur gardener?

We suggest the following practical definition:
"The growing of vegetables and soft fruits using natural environmentally friendly methods and substances including seeds, fertilisers, insecticides and herbicides, and avoiding the use of industrially manufactured chemical products that are potential hazards to people, soil and animals."

This definition is simple but its application is more complex. In practice, organic vegetable growing can be practised at a number of levels.

LEVEL 1 - USE NATURAL FERTILISERS AND MAXIMISE SOIL IMPROVEMENT BY WORMS.

Use well-rotted garden compost, farmyard manure and seaweed from the seashore after a storm. Resist using compound chemical fertilisers, especially the nitrates that leach into the water table.

Concentrate on feeding the soil and adding humus that attracts and stimulates worms. Avoid using mechanical ploughs and tillers. Recognise that light digging, raking and worm activity can be just as effective and don't compact the soil.

Help plants seek out and extract the natural chemicals and trace elements they need by feeding with infusions of comfrey and nettles. See Chapters 56 and 76 for details.

Benefits: Low cost, safe, keeps garden, local animal sheds and stables tidy. Builds up a friable soil and prevents erosion.

LEVEL 2 - NO USE OF MANUFACTURED CHEMICAL INSECTICIDES.

But use ancient herbal sprays such as infusions of horsetail, garlic, and tobacco plus derris, which is a natural product. Avoid hazardous chemical sprays.

Benefits: Low cost and safe.

LEVEL 3 - NO USE OF MANUFACTURED CHEMICAL HERBICIDES TO CONTROL WEEDS.

If you garden organically, you will not have a weed-free vegetable plot because the soil is rich and attractive to all seeds. Inevitably, hours will be spent hoeing and hand weeding. In fact some weeds are beneficial companion plants or useful as sprays. Weeds can also be suppressed by mulches and plastic or cardboard around plants, covered with soil to disguise and hold them down.

Benefits: Exercise, inexpensive, safer to people and animals.

LEVEL 4 - THE PLANTING OF ORGANIC SEEDS.

Purchase and plant seeds from the extensive European seed bank of the older varieties of vegetables pre-industrial generic modification or save your own seeds from year to year. Unfortunately, organic seeds may cost a little more. But this is more than compensated by vegetables designed for direct domestic consumption and not the specialist farmer, canner, freezer or supermarket, pre-packed.

Benefits: Fresh daily vegetables of the size, taste, colour, bite and quality that you choose. No manufactured chemicals on the surface of the seeds or vegetables.

LEVEL 5 - THE DEVELOPMENT AND MANAGEMENT OF THE VEGETABLE PLOT AS A BALANCED, NATURALLY OCCURRING ECOLOGICAL SYSTEM.

We started with a weed-covered plot untilled for five years. We have been amazed at the beneficial companion plants and animal kingdom that can evolve within a few years. Often without conscious pre-planning intervention. Our vegetable gardening is now as diverse and interesting as it was helping grandfathers 50 years ago! We have recycled to the days of the mixed cottage garden and vegetable huerta worked by donkeys and mules before villagers could afford mechanical ploughs and chemicals. Bright flowers attract pollinators and make the plot a pleasure to work in. Flowering plants and herbs are also part of our beneficial companion planting system. The natural food-chains produced by our resident population of aphids, beetles, snails, grasshoppers, frogs, snakes and birds has done wonders in decimating the first year's battle with bugs.

Benefits: Less work in the long run, diversity of plants and wild life, continuous rebuilding of a previously overworked, undernourished soil. An interesting place in which to potter.

We hope that more readers will be stimulated to grow vegetables organically, or, a better adjective, naturally.

58. Annual vegetable garden review

It is important to evaluate the successes and failures of the past year before preparing a planting plan for the next autumn and spring sowings and buying new seeds.

We have split the review into two parts. Firstly an identification of problems and possible solutions. Secondly an evaluation of how ecological/organic your vegetable gardening practices have become.

Both are presented as questionnaires to make the annual review objective.

REVIEW OF SUCCESSES AND FAILURES

What crops were the greatest success in terms of yield and quality of produce?	1. .... 2. .... 3.	What did you change in your basic vegetable growing practices during the last year compared to previous years?	1. .... 2. .... 3. ....
What crops were the greatest failure in terms of yield and quality of produce?	1. .... 2. .... 3.	Were the same crops successful or failures the previous year?	Yes No Partially
What were the main problems with the poorer crops compared to the best?	1. .... 2. .... 3.	From the above analysis could any of the differences or changes in gardening practice explain why you had failures?	1. .... 2. .... 3. ....
Were there any basic differences in the way you produced the best and poorest crops? E.g. seeds, situation, weather, watering, feeds, diseases, sprays, shade, etc.	1. .... 2. .... 3.	What changes in gardening practice should you consider for next autumn and spring plantings?	1. .... 2. .... 3. ....

REVIEW OF ECOLOGICAL/ORGANIC PRACTICES

Issue	CURRENT PERSONAL PRACTICES	SCORE FOR ANSWER	PERSONAL SCORE
1. Natural/ecological enrichment and improvement of soil	Only use proprietary chemical fertilisers Use the above plus peat and substitutes Now use some compost and have cut back on chemical fertilisers by half Use rotted manure and compost but some material may have been grown non-organically Only use well rotted manure and compost from organic sources and seashore seaweed	0 1 2 3 4	
2. Natural/ecological plant feeds during growing season	Only use proprietary chemical feeds Use above but started to use proprietary organic feeds Now use mainly proprietary or our own organic feeds Use only liquid manure and comfrey but not sure that all manure is organic Only use natural liquid organic manure, comfrey, nettles and seaweed	0 1 2 3 4	
3. Natural/ecological herbicides to control weeds	Use only proprietary chemical products Above plus some hand picking/hoeing Hand pick, hoe, mulch, but still use herbicides in the spring Hand pick, hoe and compost Only hand pick, hoe or mulch, plus plastic and carpet smothering	0 1 2 3 4	
4. Natural/ecological insecticides and companion planting	Still use chemical sprays: No companion planting 80% chemical 20% natural: Starting companion planting 50% chemical 50% natural: Substantial companion planting 20% chemical 80% natural: Major companion planting Only natural plant based sprays and sulphur: Full companion planting	0 1 2 3 4	
5. Use of ecologically/organically produced/protected seeds	Continue to use regular seeds Regular seeds + 20% organic seeds Regular seeds + 50% organic seeds 80% organic seeds 100% organic seeds	0 1 2 3 4	
6. Development/management of balanced natural ecological	Plot sterile. Few worms. No wildlife. Worms appearing. Beneficial wildlife starting to visit. Companion planting started. Worms breeding. Frogs, toads, ladybirds resident. Some impact from companion planting. Many worms, snakes in residence. Birds nesting nearby. Companion planting working. Plot now a haven for range of natural wildlife who control, with companion planting, most infestations. Topsoil full of worms.	0 1 2 3 4	

Observations on scores

19-24   You have become an organic gardener.
13-18   Well on the way to being an organic gardener.
7-12   A practical start to organic gardening.
0-7   No real interest in organic methods yet.

This review was produced at the request of a number of CBN readers who asked, "How do we judge whether we are organic gardeners?" We hope the review is of assistance and will perhaps encourage more readers to produce vegetables ecologically/organically or naturally.

59. Companion planting and lunar calendar

Companion planting and the lunar gardening calendar are of particular interest to the vegetable gardener but also have application in the flower garden.

Companion planting was first practised in Spain by Roman agriculturalists two millenniums ago. The art and practice has developed since by both accidental observations and scientific study. In recent years its practice has widened as many insect and plant diseases have become resistant to traditional chemicals.

So what is companion planting and how can you use it?
Companion planting is the planting of different plants in close proximity or in succession so that they stimulate each other's growth, or repel their natural enemies, which may be insects or other plants.

Thus it is very useful in the vegetable garden. For instance:
- Chives or garlic grown between rows of peas or lettuce can control aphids.
- Tomatoes grown near asparagus can keep down the asparagus beetle.
- Marigolds between cucumbers, squashes and melons can reduce the incidence of cucumber beetle.
- Onions grown either side of carrots can prevent the devastation of the carrot fly.
- Sweetcorn which needs nitrogen can be grown close to or following peas or runner beans.
- A line of roses in the vegetable plot attract important pollinators and eaters of aphids.
- And in the flower garden, chives, garlic and marigolds between roses should reduce the incidence of green and black fly.

However, there are also negatives:
- Sunflowers and sweetcorn are mutually beneficial but sunflowers should not be planted near broccoli, Brussels sprouts or cabbage.
- Thyme plants are beneficial to aubergine plants but the opposite to courgettes and squash.

The subject is complex since plants can help each other in many ways. These include:
1. The repelling of harmful insects or attracting them away from other plants.
2. The support of insect populations which are beneficial to other plants as pollinators, predators or parasites.
3. By improving the soil by mineral accumulation, humus addition or providing green manure.

At the same time, some plants are harmful to others through competition for trace elements, root and leaf secretions, or a perfume that puts off pollinators. If you are interested in knowing more about the subject then look out for a specialist book or chart. An excellent chart was produced by Michael Littlewood (Tel/Fax 00 44 1984 641330).

Planting by the lunar calendar was practised by North American Indians and ancient Egyptians. Like companion planting, it developed first by observant but accidental observations, spread by folklore, and was then subject to more scientific study by monks in the Middle Ages.

The theory is that:
a. There are good and bad times during the month and year for planting seeds and plants, and gathering crops.
b. These times are determined by the life cycle of the moon, the height of the moon in the sky and the prominence of the various zodiac signs. The latter makes things complex, so we will concentrate on the two other aspects.

Well-known folklore passed down from generation to generation has led to the traditional planting of potatoes on St Patrick's Day and broad beans on All Saints Day and harvest with the September harvest moon. Amazingly, these traditions tie in with the lunar calendar.

This suggests that various activities in the garden are best done during specific phases of the moon. The following are examples that we have found work.

THE GROWING MOON - NEW MOON AND BEGINNING OF FIRST QUARTER
Avoid planting during the first two days of the New Moon. Then plant seeds and plants that produce leaf crops. For example, lettuce, leeks, spinach and endives. Also, seeds for herbs and flowering plants.

SECOND QUARTER OF MOON - THE GROWING MOON
Plant vegetables that produce fruits above the ground. For example, beans, peas, squash, watermelon.

THE WANING MOON - FULL MOON BEGINNING OF THE THIRD QUARTER
Plant seeds and transplant seedlings that produce crops under the ground. For instance, potatoes, radish, carrots and beetroot. This time is also suggested for planting bulbs, trees and sunflowers.

FOURTH QUARTER OF MOON
Not considered an ideal planting time. But good for digging, removing weeds and cutting back excessive growth of shrubs.

A more detailed examination of the Calendar then indicates that the position of the moon in the sky has an additional impact. So as a refinement it suggests that green vegetables are best picked when the moon is ascending in the sky and that root crops such as potatoes are best picked for long storage when the moon is descending in the sky.

We find the indicators useful but obviously it is little use following them unless we have developed a healthy soil and water plants appropriately. If you are interested in finding out more, look out for a lunar calendar applicable to Spain. The best one we have discovered is Calendar Lunar, published by Artus Porta.

60. *Crop rotation*

Crop rotation is important if you wish to produce high yields of healthy vegetables year after year. For instance if potatoes, beans or cauliflowers were grown year after year in the same part of the vegetable plot, the quality and yields of our crops would soon deteriorate.

The deterioration is caused by disease, reduction in soil fertility and the soil becoming stale. Systematic crop rotation is practised by wise vegetable gardeners to overcome the problems. The various groups of vegetables are grown in a different part of the vegetable garden each year on a systematic three or four year cycle depending on the crops grown.

The benefits of crop rotation are fivefold.
1. A reduction in the probability of build-ups of soil-bound pests and diseases and eventual soil sickness, e.g. club root in cauliflowers, eelworm and wireworm in potatoes and carrots.
2. The gradual build-up and use of soil fertility. Increased fertility is achieved by the addition of manure and compost and the natural soil enrichment properties of crops such as peas, e.g.

 - *the heavy application of manure for squashes and potatoes. The latter will also aerate and break down the soil and smother perennial weeds. Less manure then needs to be added for follow-on crops for a number of planting seasons.*

 - *peas and beans add nitrogen to the soil. This is of benefit to follow-on planting of nitrogen-hungry crops such as cauliflowers and Brussels sprouts.*

3. The different methods of soil cultivation required for different vegetables can be segregated, lightening the preparation work each year, e.g.

 - *easily prepared lazy ridges for potatoes and square flooded beds for melons.*

4. The benefits of companion planting can be maximised year after year. We discussed this important topic in the previous chapter, e.g.

 - *carrots benefit from being planted with onions. Tomatoes react negatively to being planted near brassicas (e.g. cauliflowers and broccoli).*

5. An optimum distribution of irrigation, spray or hosed water is achieved, e.g.

 - *potatoes need less watering than beans. Melons (except water melons) need less water than pumpkins or courgettes.*

A practical grouping of vegetables for crop rotation purposes is as follows. The groups are listed in the sequence of crop rotation.

	TYPICAL VEGETABLES
1.	Potatoes - early and main-crop
2.	Root crops - carrots, parsnips, radishes
3.	Onions - leeks, onions, garlic
4.	Fruits - sweet peppers, aubergines, tomatoes
5.	Legumes - peas, beans
6.	Brassicas - cauliflowers and broccoli
7.	Squashes

The favourable climate of the northern and inland areas allows vegetables to be grown all year. The above sequence is therefore complete every four years.

What this means in practice is illustrated below.

	PLOT AREA/VEGETABLE GROUP						
Planting Time	**A**	**B**	**C**	**D**	**E**	**F**	**G**	**H**
Spring - Year 1	1	2	3	4	5	6	7	-
Autumn - Year 1	2	3	-	5	6	-	-	1
Spring - Year 2	2	3	4	5	6	7	-	1
Autumn - Year 2	3	-	5	6	-	-	1	2

Since squashes do not like growing near potatoes, the plot is left fallow for six months before commencing the next cycle with potatoes.

Other crops, if grown, can be slotted into the planting pattern in accordance with their positive companion planting affinities

 e.g. - a. sweetcorn near beans
 - b. lettuce near tomatoes and carrots but away from broccoli and fennel.

Asparagus is, of course, a vegetable that doesn't fit in with the idea of normal crop rotation. The asparagus bed should, therefore, be planted in a corner of the plot away from the mainstream crops. However, asparagus plants don't last forever. It is therefore advantageous to plant new beds from seed or cuttings also on a four-year cycle. Move asparagus beds every eight years.

Now is a good time to compare your own practices over recent years with the above chart. Work out a practical plan for phasing into the cycle over the next two planting seasons.

61. Soil testing and improvement

Soil testing is important in the vegetable garden, before taking steps to improve the soil. A series of tests will help you to prepare and maintain the soil for autumn plantings. Further tests in the spring will help you maintain a continuous soil improvement programme.

There are two important approaches to soil testing. Firstly, physically look at and feel your soil. Secondly, more scientific chemical testing. Before purchasing a test kit and have an afternoon of fun with the test tube, ask yourself the following questions about the soil in the vegetable plot.

(1) How did vegetables grow during the spring and summer? Which vegetables grew the best and worst? Were there definite areas of the vegetable plot that did well and others poorly?

(2) Could the difference of success by explained by:

(a) Differences in drainage. Some areas of soil being light and friable and others clinging and clay-like. Do you need to improve the drainage system or the texture of some areas by digging in considerable areas of organic matter and sand to lighten the soil?

(b) The proximity of the plants to each other. Did your planting pattern achieve positive impacts or negative impacts between plants? We considered companion planting in some detail in Chapter 59. Positive and negative impacts could include:
Positive Impacts: Onions alongside carrots. Spinach alongside broad beans.
Negative Impacts: Potatoes alongside courgettes. Tomatoes alongside broccoli.

(c) Has your sequence of planting been beneficial? We looked at crop rotation in Chapter 60. A good crop of beans may have been the result of planting where peppers, onions and carrots had been grown the previous autumn and plenty of well-rotted compost had been dug in two months before planting seeds. A poor crop of spring broccoli and cauliflower may have been caused by not planting where peas and beans had been grown before thus creating essential nitrogen in the soil.

(d) Too much or too little sun.

(e) A wind-blown unsheltered position.

(f) Chemical blown over from a neighbouring plot.

(g) Planting seeds or plants too early or too late.

Consider the pattern of your answers and consider what basic improvements can be made for the next season's sowings and plantings. Next, buy a soil testing kit at a local gardening shop or have one brought from Northern Europe with instructions in your own language.

You will find that even the basic kits enable you to test soil samples speedily for five things: acidity/alkalinity, lime deficiency, phosphorous deficiency, potash deficiency, humus deficiency.

To understand your vegetable plot, take samples from each corner and a network of intermediate points on the vegetable plot. Prepare a chart and number the samples carefully so that the results don't get mixed up. If you prepare a large plan of the vegetable plot, you can also write the results on the plan. This will help you to decide what action to take as a result of the tests.

Normally, the acidity/alkalinity is tested first by the pH test. pH is an abbreviation for the "hydrogen ion concentration" in the moisture in the soil. This creates the resultant acidity/alkalinity. Measurement is on a 0-14 scale, 0 is very acid and 14 very alkaline and 7 neutral. In general, vegetables grow best with a pH between 6.5 and 7.0. But, naturally, some plants thrive better than others in an acid soil.

However, the change of a single unit is a 10-fold difference. For instance, a pH of 6 indicates an acidity level 10 times greater than a neutral soil. Potatoes will love such soil but few other vegetables will. Cabbages, for instance, need a neutral soil. If necessary, a soil can be made more acid by adding a raw mixture of sulphate and ammonia.

Cauliflower, Brussels sprouts and other brassica vegetables thrive in a lime-rich soil, as do peas and beans. If the lime test is too low then add lime in autumn, being careful not to get it on any leaves. Preferably, it should be done a month or two before planting. Sulphur can also be used to reduce alkalinity and has health benefits as well. Lime does three things. Balances the acidity of the soil, breaks up clinging clay soils and helps plants unlock the nutritional content of the soil.

The importance of the other tests are as follows:

- Nitrogen is essential to help plants grow, it stimulates their green colour and develops leaves and stems.
- Phosphates stimulate early growth, strong root systems, the evolution of mature plants and flowering.
- Potash helps plants resist disease and cope with variations in weather conditions. It stimulates starch content and cell wall strength. It is also essential for crispness, colour, flavour and stimulation of fruit and vegetables.

A balance of all three is therefore essential to the growing of good vegetables. But first, it is important to recognise the varying needs of different vegetable groups.

Element	High content required by	Medium content required by	Low content required by
Nitrogen	Potatoes Leeks Beetroot Spinach Broccoli	Courgettes French beans Lettuce Onions Leeks	Broad beans Carrots Parsnips Radish Peas
Phosphate	Spinach Lettuce Purslane Rocket Asparagus	Broad beans Carrots French beans Onions Potatoes	Brussels sprouts Peas Radish Leeks
Potash	Spinach Pumpkins Courgettes Strawberries Artichokes	Broad beans Leeks Onions Potatoes Beetroot	Brussels sprouts Carrots Cabbage Lettuce Peas

Now that we understand the quality of our soil and the needs of vegetables, we now have an important decision to make. Shall we improve our soil naturally or chemically? Some typical fertilisers and their properties are summarised in the following chart:

Fertiliser	Impact on crops	Typical content			
		Nitrogen	Phosphate	Potash	Trace elements
Farmyard manure	Slow	Low/med.	Low	Low	Low
Infusions of manure	Medium	High	Medium	Medium	Low
Seaweed	Slow	Low	-	Low	High
Chicken manure	Medium	Low	Low	Low	Low
Bone meal	Slow	Low	High	Low	Low
Wood ash	Medium	Low	Low	High	Low
Potassium nitrate	Quick	High	-	Very high	-
Sulphate of ammonia	Quick	High	-	-	-
Sulphate of potash	Medium	-	-	Very high	-
Super phosphate	Medium	-	High	-	-
Balanced fertiliser	High	High	High	High	Low

From the above table it is obvious that many barrow-loads of farmyard manure and seaweed will be required to achieve the same chemical input as a tub of chemical fertiliser. However, manure also provides the humus required to produce the light loam needed for healthy plants. Also, the chemicals will build up season-by-season and not washed away by gota frías or be a burning concentration in dry weather. The gradual build-up will have medium and long term benefits on the soil and surrounding environment, most importantly natural fertilisers will produce tasty, crisp crops that, in many cases, will mature over a number of weeks.

The heavy use of chemical fertilisers and copious water will certainly produce quick-growing, large plants. But there is a risk that they may be watery and lack taste. Often, all plants mature together leading to a short picking season.

This is fine for supermarket suppliers but is it what you prefer? Also, the long-term excessive use of nitrates can leach out into the underlying water table, making water undrinkable due to the nitrate content.

The choice is yours. We prefer the organic approach as discussed in Chapters 57 and 76. Naturally, soil testing will also be of benefit in the flower garden.

62. Snails

The control of snails in the flower and vegetable garden is a vital activity. Few of our gardens in Spain are without snails, often a considerable number and sometimes of large, edible size. Luckily, we are generally much less bothered by slugs than in Northern Europe.

Unfortunately, snails seek out young seedlings and succulent sappy stems and leaves to feed on, especially in the summer months. They can appear from nowhere after a watering or shower of rain. So, how can we control them?

The following 10 ideas should help. But we suggest you use two or three methods in combination.

1. Collect them by hand. Many young children will gladly help out for a bounty. But watch your pricing. It may turn out to be an expensive activity. Once collected you have a number of possibilities.

a. Take them into the country and release them on a well-vegetated hillside away from gardens or smallholdings.

b. Keep a few as pets for snail races!

c. Select the large ones and put in a snail cage. Feed them on rosemary cuttings for two weeks to clean them out. Place in a covered container overnight in 3cms of salty water. Rinse, then cook for immediate use or freeze.

d. Drown or squash them, but you may not find this humane.

2. Place one metre squares of cardboard at strategic points in the flower and vegetable garden. Dampen the soil underneath and weight the cardboard down with a rock. This often acts as a magnet for snails. Lift up the sheets regularly and deal with snails as above.

3. Stick canes into the ground a few feet from vulnerable plants. Snails, small ones especially, climb and stick to the canes probably drinking the water that condenses on the polished surface overnight. Again, collect them every few days.

4. Put a ring of sharp material round young, tender plants, such as: gravel, crushed nut or eggshells, or prickly oak leaves. The snails won't slide over them.

5. Place a circle of comfrey leaves around emerging/young seedlings. The snails seem to prefer the comfrey. We use this to protect young lettuce and melon plants with significant success

6. Make simple traps by sinking plastic beakers into the ground and filling with beer. Unfortunately, our experience is that Spanish snails are not as heavy beer drinkers as in the UK!

7. Put a few cabbage leaves under the grill for a few minutes, but don't burn. Place them along suspected snail paths. Snails will be attracted by the smell during dark. But you will have to go with a torch to collect them.

8. Put waste lettuce leaves in a heap and thoroughly dampen the ground. Then collect the snails as for No 7.

9. Use proprietary snail bait pellets to attract and kill snails. But don't over use. The dead snails are poisonous to reptiles, birds and hedgehogs. As a poison they are dangerous to young children if they attempt to collect the attractive green pellets. Cover them with a slab of rock supported on a stone if you anticipate this problem.

10. Purchase one of the proprietary snail traps. There are a wide variety advertised in gardening magazines these days. Only your trials will demonstrate whether they are value for money. Some traps now use biological control methods such as nematodes. Nematodes that get into the bodies of snails and live on them. How successful they are or what side effects they have we don't know but plan to find out.

We hope that the above ideas will lead to fewer losses of carefully raised seedlings and plants in both the vegetable and flower gardens.

63. Tomatoes

Tomatoes are one of the easiest and most useful vegetables to grow on the Mediterranean. Seeds sown in February can fruit from June to December and even through to the following February with a mild winter and regular feeding. A wide variety of seeds and plants are readily available in garden centres, horticultural shops and markets. We look at the raising of tomatoes from seed, planting out, ongoing care and harvesting.

1. RAISING TOMATOES FROM SEED

a. For continuous crops plant a few seeds every two weeks from February to April.

b. We find the following procedure the most successful.
- Fill a multicell or a normal seed tray with dampened compost and spray with an ecological fungicide.
- Plant several seeds to a cell. You can thin plants out later if necessary.
- If planting a number of varieties, label well!
- If still cold, cover trays with a large sheet of clear plastic to create a sealed microclimate.
- Place in a semi shaded position.
- If well sealed, the microclimate will keep the seedlings damp and you will not have to water.
- To make watering easier and to retain heat we place the multicell trays inside a polystyrene fish box with three centimetres of damp potting compost in the base.
- Remove the plastic when the plantlets have four leaves.
- Harden off in a semi shaded area to prepare for planting out.

c. If you plant in normal seed trays you will need to separate and plant on the seedlings. Crowded plants can become stunted and the leaves turn yellow.
- Pot on seedlings at the first or second leaf stage to six-centimetre pots or peat pots. Use a good well-draining compost. Keep moist. Watering from the base works well if you stand the pots in trays of damp compost. It encourages strong roots.

2. PLANTING OUT

- Early plants can be planted out in March. However in many areas they will need protection from chilly nights and strong winds.
- If plantlets are leggy, plant deep to reduce the length of stem below the first leaves.
- Plant in soil enriched with well-rotted manure, grass cuttings and seaweed.
- Put a small piece of fresh nettle in each planting hole for extra nitrogen.
- To keep roots damp and reduce weed growth, plant through holes in black plastic, or mulch around the stems.
- Tie each plant to a cane with soft raffia or plastic ties.
- If you have more than 10 plants, construct a strong cane planting frame to protect plants from strong winds.
- Rotate where you plant each year. Generally tomatoes follow onions and root crops. Tomatoes are hungry feeders and leave few nutrients in the soil.
- Companion plant with onions, garlic, leeks, carrots or celery.
- Do not plant alongside potatoes.

3. FEEDING TOMATO PLANTS

- In seed trays and when first planted out, feed with a dilute liquid comfrey/nettle feed or a proprietary tomato feed every 10 days.
- When first flowers appear, feed twice a week with liquid comfrey (high in potash), or use a proprietary tomato feed.
- Do not feed with liquid nettle - nitrogen - once the plants are fruiting.

4. WATERING

- Tomatoes do not like irregular watering.
- Just keep young plants damp before flowering.
- A drip watering system can be very useful if you have a convenient piped water supply.
- Water well just as the first flowers appear and then just once a week and likewise throughout the fruiting season.
- Always water at the base.

5. TYPICAL PROBLEMS

The most common problems are:-
- Botrytis fungus, which causes the fruit to fall early. Caused by careless splashing of soil on lower leaves when watering.
- Mildews - a grey mould on underside of leaves. Mainly occurs in humid weather after storms. Use sulphur to prevent and to treat the above. Put the powder in a sock and dust the plants early in the morning. You can also spray with horsetail. Spray plants and soil and repeat every two weeks. An alternative is to cut 8-10cm lengths of copper wire and wind around the stem. The copper in contact with the plant emits ions which protects it against all fungal infections.
- Splitting of tomatoes while ripening. This is caused by irregular watering which creates a "start-stop" growth. As with all plants the best disease deterrent is to plant healthy plants in healthy soil. Note that the largest seedlings are not always the strongest.

6. HARVESTING AND STORING

- Pick tomatoes before they become overripe.
- Remove rotting fruit to prevent spread of disease.
- Make chutneys, pickles or freeze for soups, etc.
- In a mild winter tomatoes can continue fruiting until February if you leave in a few strong plants in the autumn.
- There is a Spanish variety called colgar which can be stored. They are picked in July/August just before they are fully ripe. Hung up in trusses in a dry shaded airy place, they will keep fresh and juicy in the right conditions through to late autumn/early winter. When growing this variety do not over water or over feed with nitrogen as either will reduce their storing properties.

We hope that the above ideas help to produce good yields over many months.

64. Onions, leeks and garlic

Onions are an important Spanish vegetable family. Even a small patch is rewarding. We look at the raising or purchase of plantlets or sets, the preparation of soil, planting out, growing to maturity, harvesting and storage.

1. RAISING OR PURCHASE OF PLANTLETS OR SETS

VEGETABLE	GROW FROM	PLANT	HARVEST
Chives	Seeds	Feb/Mar	June/Nov
	Plantlets	Feb/Mar	April/Nov
Garlic	Cloves from those bought for cooking	Jan/Mar Oct/Nov-storing	Young while growing Aug for drying
Onions	Seeds	Aug/Sept non-storing	May July
	Seeds	Jan/Feb storing Transplant April/May	August onwards
	Plantlets	Nov/Jan non-storing	May/July
	Plantlets	March/May storing	August onwards
	Sets	Jan/Feb	August onwards
Salad onions	Seeds	Feb/Mar	Spring/Summer
Leeks	Seeds	Jan/Feb under plastic Transplant May July transplant Sept/Oct	July/August onwards May/Jun August onwards Late winter/early spring

Onion plantlets are available widely in bunches of two or three hundred.

PREPARATION OF SOIL

Onions like soils enriched with well rotted manure and a dusting of wood ash.

PLANTING TIPS

a. Seeds - Onions and Leeks.
For early onions and leeks, plant seeds in a seed tray or polystyrene fish box. Seal with plastic to create a moist microclimate. When strong, harden off and transplant.
For later sowings, scatter seeds evenly in a square bed surrounded by a ridge. Keep moist by gently flooding the bed. Do not disturbing the delicate new plants. Transplant when about the length of a biro.

b. Onion Sets
Plant by pushing them gently into moist soil leaving the growing tip just above the surface.

c. Garlic
The red variety is better for storing. Select only the large outside cloves for planting. Push into well-prepared damp soil. Plant three to five centimetres deep, leaving the point just above the soil. Allow 12-15cm between each clove and 20-30cm between each row.

d. Plantlets - Onions
When planting, cut off top four centimetres of green to encourage roots. Dib four centimetre deep holes. Insert plant. Water in so that the roots settle in with no air gaps. For ease of watering prepare a square bed surrounded by a ridge or plant on a raised bed. The alternative is a drip system.

e. Leeks
Follow instructions as above but plant deeper. There need be only a small piece of plant showing. Water in each plant and allow to settle in on its own. Earth up the stems to encourage longer whiter stems. Leeks take much longer to mature than onions. But they are easy to grow. We plant regularly throughout the year. They don't appear to have any particular problems. Those planted in summer can be left in the ground over winter/spring to give you a continuous crop. Allow a few to go to seed to give you a supply of seeds for the next year.

GROWING TO MATURITY

a. Watering
Onions/leeks/chives - *seedlings* - keep moist.
Transplants - water well in first few weeks to encourage growth. Then only when there are long dry spells. Do not over water onions when they are near maturity - they may rot.
Garlic - likes to be kept moist until the first shoots appear. Thereafter they prefer to be kept on the dry side.

b. Feeding
If planted in a previously well-manured site they should not need a lot of extra feeding. Monthly we feed all members of the onion family (except garlic) with a mixture of liquid manure, comfrey and nettle. Garlic does not need to be fed.

c. Spraying
If onion fly appear make up a spray of tomato shoots by infusing tomato leaves in boiling water, cool, strain and spray onions.
Garlic can suffer from fungal diseases. This is caused by too wet soil or too much fresh manure. Rust can also be a problem - spray with liquid seaweed.

d. Weeding
Weed regularly and keep the soil loose and well aerated.

e. Mulching
As they like a well aerated soil they prefer not to be mulched. Sometimes early onions are planted through plastic sheeting and watered profusely. They are good for salads but will not store well.

HARVESTING AND STORAGE

1. Chives - Cut as required. Cut them to stop them from going to seed.
2. Garlic - You can pick garlic planted Jan-March while it is still growing, before the leaves turn yellow. Those planted in October, if you want larger bulbs, flatten over yellowing stems and leave to dry in the sun in the spring. Pull up and plait in bunches. Hang in sunny well-aerated, dry place. When dry store in a dry, shady place.
3. Onions -Earlier varieties pick to eat. Later varieties, when they have reached full size (usually around end July/August), bend over tops and allow to dry off. Pull up and lay on trays or sacks in a shady, well-aerated place. Leave until they are completely dry. Store in bunches or hang in open sacks in a dark, well-ventilated place.
4. Salad onions - Pick for eating as required.
5. Leeks - Dig up as required.

We hope these guidelines help you produce good onions in a corner of the garden.

65. Marrows and squashes

The marrow, pumpkin and squash families include a number of useful and interesting vegetables. All are varieties of the curbita species. Some more useful in the kitchen and others more useful for decorative purposes. They are frequently and easily grown in Spain, where the hot summer ensures quick growing fruit and maturity before autumn temperatures drop. We grow the following for the purposes indicated.

- **Pumpkins** - for use in thickening soups and as a base for pumpkin pie and pumpkin bread.
- **Squashes** - a smaller sweeter pumpkin for baking in the oven or steaming. Round and long violin version are both good eaten as a tasty vegetable, also for making Halloween lanterns. Ready for picking in August. They store well in a cool dark cellar or garage until May.
- **Marrows** - for storing and cooking stuffed with meat or fish fillings as a starter or main course.
- **Courgettes** - both long and round varieties as a steamed or lightly fried vegetable.
- **Gourds** - as interesting colourful decorations for the terrace and table.

With a little care they are easy to grow on the Costa, provided they are regularly watered and fed. They love the hot summer sun.

SO WHAT ARE THE SUCCESS FACTORS?

1. Buy good seeds or keep seeds from large tasty or decorative produce from the previous year. Remove the seeds before cooking, dry in the sun for a few weeks and then store in an airtight container until the following March. Look out for the Halloween range of seeds that impressed us at the Eurogarden Exhibition in Valencia and in use.
2. Plant seeds in pots from mid February to April to produce strong plantlets for planting out in late April or May.
3. Plant seeds two or three to a pot and select the strongest plantlets for eventual planting out.
4. Plant in 10 to 15cm pots and germinate/grow in a warm garden frame or a large plastic bag.
5. Fill the pots with a friable mix of soil, well-rotted manure and compost.
6. Once the seeds germinate and two leaves appear feed the plantlets weekly with a dilute liquid feed. We use a manure/comfrey mix.
7. In late April or early May plant the plantlets out in sunny positions, protected if possible from strong drying winds. If not already done in February/March dig half metre round planting holes 25cm deep and fill with a 1:1 soil/rotted manure. Mix well. Water and plant the plantlets ensuring that the total stem up to the first leaves is below soil level. In reality the more manure and compost you can use the better.
8. Place a circle of comfrey leaves, wood ash, or prickly evergreen oak leaves around the plant to inhibit hungry snails and slugs. We prefer these ecological solutions to the use of slug pellets that kill off useful insects, animals and birds as well as the slugs.
9. If you live in the inland valleys cover the newly planted plantlets with a cloche. An inexpensive version 25cm x 25cm and 10cm high can be produced from scrap wood covered with heavy clear plastic. Watch out for snakes that find such warm "hothouses" good temporary homes for mating!
10. Do not remove the cloches until:-

a) warm spring days are the norm and the cold winds have gone.

b) the plantlets have strong stems and four to six leaves depending on the variety of vegetable being grown.

11. Water and feed regularly if it does not rain for a period of seven days. These vegetables must have moist soil around the roots at all time for success.
12. To prevent weeds and retain moisture cover the planting ridge or bed with a sheet of black plastic before planting plantlets and plant through a 20cm circular or square hole.
13. All types of squash and marrow are susceptible to mildew and fungal attack in warm humid weather. It is therefore wise to dust leaves with natural sulphur powder every fortnight. A good tip is to put it in a sock and shake lightly. Always dust early morning or late evening. Wear goggles. A spray of the herb horsetail also helps.
14. All these vegetables spread. Especially pumpkins whose lateral branches can grow from 10 to 20 metres under ideal conditions. They therefore need to be allotted a large area away from other vegetables. When plants are 50cm long pinch out the end to stimulate branches.
15. The smaller decorative gourds can however be grown as trailing specimens on rockeries, up fences or in large terrace pots. Gourds come in a wide range of shapes, sizes and colours. They include five to 10cm round or oblong green or yellow, single, mixed or striped colours. Some smooth and some nobbled. Also the larger bottle shapes were traditionally used as water containers by travellers and pilgrims.
16. Ensure that all plants are kept moist with regular watering and feeding to stimulate a long fruiting period.
17. Normally pollination is no problem. However, if you have many flowers but no fruit forming, try hand pollination from cut male flowers to the female flowers.
18. The harvesting practices vary. For instance: -

Courgettes are best picked young and frequently, leaving just a few fruits to mature for winter storage. For instance courgettes are tastiest when 10 to 15cm long but left for a week or two they will produce 40cm monsters for storage and winter eating or preparation of chutneys especially in September/October when you have a glut of tomatoes and peppers.

Squash fruits are best picked for storage when the leaves of the plants have died back. Similarly for the large pumpkins. If you want competition-size pumpkins leave only one fruit on each plant. Healthy squashes will store for 10 months. We cut and shared out our prize pumpkin, a 60kg giant grown totally organically!

19. When the best fruits are cut for cooking, retain the seeds. Dry in the sun and store in airtight containers as self-grown organic/ecological seeds for the next year.

20. Within your crop rotation system, pumpkins, squashes, courgettes and melons are best planted to follow or precede potatoes.

21. With regard to companion planting, pumpkins, squashes and gourds respond well to adjacent planting of nasturtiums, radish, fennel and sweet corn and negatively to close planting of potatoes.

We hope you enjoy good vegetables all the year round. Squashes will keep till the following June, by which time new courgettes will be ready to harvest.

66. *Asparagus*

Asparagus can be easily grown, especially in the cooler inland valleys. Freshly cut thick asparagus are very tasty. Much more so than many of the several days old bunches often seen in supermarkets or the best quality tinned or jarred versions very popular in restaurants. But you need to be a patient gardener. For success you will have to wait three years before cutting your first crop apart from the odd "taster". If you are still interested October is the time to start preparing the bed.

OBTAINING PLANTS

Look out for packets or bunches of plants or crowns over the next few months. They are available on the southern Costas but not to the same extent as in Northern Spain. If you are making an autumn tour in Northern Spain or France look for them in the markets or ask in your hostel whether you could obtain plants in the village. Even if you only obtain a dozen plants as we did initially, it is a start. In April it is possible to plant seed to obtain strong plantlets to plant out the following autumn. Germination is easy.

PREPARING THE SOIL

Traditionally asparagus is grown on raised beds some 25-30cms above the surrounding area. It is worth preparing the bed well as asparagus beds may crop for 20 years. First remove all perennial weeds. Second make trenches 20cm deep by 20cm wide. Line the bottom with 10cm of compost or manure and then fill in with soil. Allow 50cm between plants and rows to allow the crowns when planted ample room to develop planting out.

Plant out crowns purchased during autumn or winter as follows. Plant as soon as obtained to prevent them drying out. If they are dry when you obtain them soak them in water for 24 hours before planting. Dig a hole wider than the circumference of the roots and 10cm deep. Spread out the roots, fill in carefully with soil and firm. Mark the position of each crown with a cane. Then cover the raised bed with a five centimetre mulch of compost or manure. Naturally seed raised plants can be planted out similarly next autumn.

PATIENCE

For the next two years keep the bed moist, mulched and weed free. Resist the undoubted temptation to cut the first asparagus as they push through the ground in March/April for the first two years. Allow the spears to grow into fern like foliage. Leave this to die back in the autumn. Unless the sap goes down to the roots each autumn strong plants will not develop. Cutting the attractive ferns for adding to flowers will take away the vital natural food supply to the roots. However if the fern starts to go to seed snip off the forming flowers.

THE FIRST HARVEST

You will be rewarded for your efforts in the third spring. As the asparagus shoots appear, cut no more than two or three shoots per plant. More patience! Yes, but the benefits will be stronger and stronger crops to cut in the 15 or more years following. Like a wine cellar an asparagus bed might be a good investment for the next generation.

ONGOING CARE

1. Keep the bed moist. Don't allow plants to dry out.
2. Top up the mulch on the bed twice a year.
3. Top up the mulch with seaweed. It is not difficult to collect from the beach after a storm. There is no need to wash the seaweed as asparagus love salt. We're told that they were originally found growing along the edge of beaches in Belgium.
4. Dust the bed with 50gms of sea salt per square metre at the end of April each year. Do it on a rainy day or water in well.
5. Spray the foliage with derris, liquid or powder during June, July and August to prevent or deter the asparagus beetle.
6. If you see holes appearing at the bottom of the foliage stems carefully dig out the grub of the asparagus fly before it bores down into the root structure.
7. Don't cut asparagus after the end of June. Leave later shoots to develop foliage.
8. Dust the foliage in July with sulphur to reduce the occurrence of rust damage.
9. Regularly weed the bed.

A good asparagus crop needs several years of patience and care. We hope your efforts are rewarded.

67. Brassicas

The brassicas family includes many varieties of useful vegetables. The most popular are cauliflowers, cabbages (red, white and savoy), broccoli (large headed and sprouting) and Brussels sprouts. In northern Spain all can be grown successfully as summer and winter crops. However along the Costas, even in the inland valleys, we find it preferable to only grow brassicas as winter/spring crops. In hotter weather they soon bolt and go to seed.

We look at how to grow each type of brassica from seed. Then we consider some common problems and solutions to them.

Naturally you can purchase brassica plantlets from nurseries or markets rather than growing them from seed.

GROWING FROM SEED

1. Cauliflowers
- Sow in seed bed direct May to June for late autumn and winter crops and July to September for winter and spring crops. We have also been successful sowing in newspaper tubes in polystyrene boxes.
- Transplant when they have five leaves.
- Plant up to the base of first leaves and be careful not to let any soil get into the centre of the plant.
- Plant 70-80cm apart. It is important to keep the soil loose and aerated around plants.
- They never like to dry out. Never water from above as it encourages fungal diseases on the forming heads.
- If the sun is still very hot when cauliflower heads start to form fold leaves over to protect them from scorching.
- They need a soil rich in humus with a high content of nitrogen and potassium. Too much nitrogen attracts bugs but to obtain nitrogen, feed with a dilute mix of liquid nettle. For potassium, feed with liquid comfrey. A mulch of comfrey leaves around the plants is very beneficial and helps retain moisture.
- Try to grow some in succession so you don't have a glut.
- A good tip if you have too many at one time is to store them for a week or two by lifting with roots. Remove surplus soil, tie together, heads down in a cool airy cellar. Spray with water regularly to keep fresh.

2. Cabbages
a. Spring cabbages
- Sow in seed bed direct from end August to end September.
- Plant on to final position mid October to mid November for picking in the spring.
- You can also plant in trays covered with plastic - January/February to transplant end February/March and April for picking end May beginning of June.

b. Autumn/winter cabbages
- Sow direct in seedbed in June, transplant July/August for picking October/December. Sow direct in seedbed in August, transplant September for picking November/February.
- Look for varieties that are suited to the various seasons.
- Transplant about 50 days after initial sowing.
- Plant 50 to 60cm apart, in well-manured soil. Keep roots well earthed up and hoe between rows. Cabbages like to be kept moist but can withstand drier conditions than cauliflowers.

3. Broccoli
There are two varieties - large headed and perpetual sprouting. Both take longer to mature than cauliflower or cabbage.
- Sow in seed bed direct April-June or in seed boxes. It is very important to sow seeds thinly. If they are too close they will become leggy and will never recover.
- Soil and feeding as for cauliflowers.
- When 10-15cm tall transplant to their final position in rows 50-60cm apart.
- Plant in moist soil that has been previously manured and firm in well.
- Keep moist and mulch with well-rotted manure and comfrey.
- They can also withstand drier conditions than cauliflowers.
- Broccoli is usually ready to pick from September onwards. Cut central head first. This will encourage side spears to form to give you a continuous delicious crop.

4. Brussels sprouts
- Sow direct in seed bed May-June.
- Transplant July/August for picking from October/March.
- Plant deeply in previously well manured soil and firm in well. This encourages more compact sprouts.
- Plant 60cm apart.
- Feed and mulch as for cauliflowers. Beware too much nitrogen produces flowery sprouts.
- They like to be regularly watered and like cauliflower, hate to be dry.
- They do not like too much sun, but can withstand -10°C - not likely on the Costas!
- Encourage a continuous crop by removing lower leaves and pick regularly.
- We prefer to pick the small Dutch sized sprout rather than when large, as is normal in the UK. The taste is better although the yield maybe lower.

PROBLEMS AND SOLUTIONS

a. A common problem is white fly. When the weather is still hot and especially after summer storms, plants can become covered with aphids and white fly.
Possible organic solutions are as follows:-
i. Spray with dilute solution of potassium soap in non-chlorinated water, or an infusion of horsetail.
ii. Put bright yellow plastic bottles between the rows - i.e. collect one-litre water bottles. Swill around yellow paint. When dry fill with water. Flies don't like the glare!
iii. Plant nasturtiums between rows. They attract white fly away from brassicas.
iv. Spray with neem, from the Asiatic plant nim - a natural insecticide.

b. Cabbage White Butterflies
i. Your plant can be destroyed overnight by an attack of caterpillars. Pick off any you see and rub off eggs.
ii. Spray with neem.
iii. Soak tomato leaves and stems in water for two hours. Spray on plants when you notice butterflies around.
c. Club root
Plant seedlings then protect with a square of felt or carpet. Cut slit on one side so that you can slide it around the base. Or cut base out of plastic pots. Slide over the plant and push into the ground to stop it blowing away.
d. Mildew.
Spray with infusion of horsetail or ecological fungicide. If spraying, spray regularly and only early in the morning.
e. Sheep, goats and horses
If any animals pass by, ensure the crop is well fenced!

We hope that the above guidelines lead to some excellent crops, if not exhibition sized heads. The latter are possible in our warm climate but they will need constant watering. And they will not taste as good as smaller more natural heads.

68. *Spaghetti*

Home grown spaghetti is a crop that could grow well in the Spanish soil and climate. With a little care, spaghetti can grow on most vegetable plots. However, sufficient water needs to be available for a good soaking every second day. It would do well fed by a grey water system from the kitchen sink. Spaghetti does not need the vast amount of water required for growing rice, such as you see in the rice fields south of Valencia. It can also be grown in large plastic pots, say 25cm diameter. They can be interesting terrace plants for children to tend. The record yield in Spain is 1.8kg per plant.

The following practical guidelines will help you achieve success.

1. Buy good quality spaghetti canes - preferably Italian. Most good delicatessens will have them in stock. Normally in 500gm packs. Look out for cream versus white canes. The latter will be too dry and difficult to germinate.
2. Don't overcrowd. A plot of four square metres will safely accommodate nine mature plants.
3. Grow plantlets during April ready for planting out in May. To ensure nine good plantlets we suggest you start off with 12 or 15. You can then plant out the strongest.
4. Prepare spaghetti canes for potting by standing them in two cm of water for 24 hours. By the lunar calendar April 1 is a good planting day so put them in water on the morning of March 31.
5. Select and clean 10cm plastic pots. Use the deep rather than shallow variety. This will help retain moisture and give ample space for a good root ball to develop.
6. Prepare the potting medium. Spaghetti grows best in a light, loamy soil as found in the fertile Po Valley in Italy. We suggest you prepare a 1:1:1 mix of well-rotted compost, good garden soil and a coarse sand. The soil is best taken from where potatoes or squash were grown last year. Dampen and fill the 10cm pots to two cm from the brim.
7. Scoop out a three cm deep hole in the centre of each pot. Plant a spaghetti cane in each. Ensure that the now soft base is curled round the bottom of the hole. This will stimulate a strong root system.
8. Set the pots in shallow trays in a sunny spot. Keep half a centimetre of water in the tray at all times for a fortnight. Ensure that the trays are kept out of the wind. Otherwise they may keel over before the root system develops.
9. By early May the plantlets should have developed several emergent side shoots with small greeny-grey leaves. Now is the time to plant out in the vegetable plot. Plant and stake as you would tomato plants. By the lunar calendar the best time for planting out will be between May 5 and 10.
10. Water and feed every two or three days. Preferably feed with an organic/ecological feed such as a comfrey or nettle infusion.
11. As the plants grow, watch out for black fly. Especially if you still have broad bean plants on the vegetable plot. Spray regularly with a garlic infusion.
12. By mid July the first crop should be ready to pick. It will probably be only 10 to 15cm long and light green in colour but the taste is exceptional. Try steaming for just a few minutes and serve with a virgin olive oil dressing.
13. The main crop should be ready to harvest by mid August. Pick when 25 to 30cm long. Lay on trays covered with kitchen paper. Place in full sun for 10 days to dry. Take indoors at night so that the drying spaghetti does not absorb overnight humidity. Alternatively dry the spaghetti in a low temperature oven.

We hope you achieve a good first crop. Success will mean that hungry visiting youngsters can be served fresh spaghetti in summer as an alternative to chips or rice. Cut into one cm lengths, home grown spaghetti is excellent for preparing fideos.

Footnote: This was first published on April 1 2001. Yes, it was April Fools Day, but we thought you would enjoy the fun!

69. Melons

Melons are relatively easy fruits to raise with the Mediterranean summer temperatures. We consider why, the selection of melons, the raising of plantlets, the care of maturing plants and harvesting.

1. WHY GROW YOUR OWN?

There are a number of advantages
1. Melons can be an interesting feature of the vegetable garden or a corner of the flower garden.
2. You can produce a selection of melons, not normally available commercially.
3. You can grow melons organically.
4. By careful harvesting, you can store and eat your own melons at Christmas.

2. SELECTION OF TYPES TO GROW

There are five main types to grow
1. Water melons - white or red fleshed. Taste variable. e.g. Moon and Stars.
2. Soft skinned ovals - yellow skinned and fleshed but not good keepers. Average taste. E.g. Amarillo Oro.
3. Hard skinned ovals - green skinned and whitish flesh - good keepers. Need to be ripe to be very juicy and enjoyable. E.g. Pinonet Piel de Sapo.
4. Cantaloupe - average sized melons, yellow or orange fleshed, perfumed and sweet, but do not store well. E.g. Sweetheart types.
5. Ogen - small to average, green to yellow in colour, very tasty, sweet and juicy. E.g. Blenheim Orange. Popular Spanish varieties will be on display in garden centres, agricultural co-operativas and horticultural shops. A selection of specialist varieties will be found in mail order catalogues including an increasing number of organic varieties.

3. RAISING PLANTS

1. Plantlets of the main Spanish varieties are often available in horticultural shops, markets and agricultural cooperatives during April and May. The first available will be water melons and the last generally ogen melons.
2. Plantlets can easily be raised from seeds. We suggest that you plant as described in Chapter 65 for marrows and squashes, but plant a month later.
3. Seeds can also be planted into the vegetable plot during May and early June.
4. For seeds and plants, prepare metre square planting positions by incorporating plenty of well-rotted manure and watering well.
5. Cantaloupe and ogens will need to be planted later than other varieties.
6. Cover plantlets and newly planted seeds with cloches, plastic sheeting around canes or square wooden boxes covered with plastic until the end of May.

4. PLANTING OUT AND ONGOING CARE

1. Dig plenty of well-rotted manure into the planting holes.
2. Follow the instructions for marrows and squashes in Chapter 65.
3. Do not plant till soil temperatures are 20ºC or more.

5. WATERING

1. Every 15 days water deeply.
2. Reduce watering when melons start to ripen. They do not need as much water as marrows and squashes.
3. Reduced watering will produce sweeter and better storing melons of all varieties.

6. OVERCOMING PROBLEMS

1. Dust with sulphur powder fortnightly - more frequently during periods of high humidity after rain, to protect from mildew and fungi.
2. Place a circle of comfrey leaves or slug pellets around young plants to protect from snails and slugs.
3. Rotate the crops so that melons are not grown on the same plot of land more frequently than once every four years. Plant after early crops of radishes or spinach.
4. Companion plant with brassicas, beans, sweetcorn, roses and borage. The latter two to attract pollinators.
5. If pollination is poor, hand-pollinate each female flower with a male flower.
6. Raise up fruit from the soil on blocks of wood, squares of cardboard or straw to prevent rotting.
7. Cover ripening melons with dried plants or straw to protect them from excess radiation from the sun.

7. PRUNING TO PRODUCE LARGE FRUITS

1. Pinch out ends of main shoots after four leaves, to stimulate fruiting side shoots.
2. Pinch out side shoots two leaves beyond the first or second forming fruits.

8. FEEDING

Feed fortnightly initially, then weekly once the fruits are formed and start to swell.

9. HARVESTING

It is not easy to determine when the ripeness of a melon is at its optimum for colour, aroma, flavour, juices or storage. Two general guidelines are:
1. Pick early for storage and keep melons for storage in a cool dark place.
2. For eating, pick when the end of the melon, where the flower was, feels soft to firm pressure, or where the connection from fruit to plant withers.

We hope these guidelines lead to tasty melons. Collect and dry seeds of especially tasty melons for planting next year. But recognise that hybrids are unlikely to reproduce faithfully.

70. Establishing an orchard

If you are interested in growing your own fruit an orchard can be anything from two trees to 200 trees. The governing factors are: How much land do you have available? Do you have inexpensive agricultural water? Are you prepared to spend time planting, watering, spraying, pruning and fruit picking?

Those of us with an 800 to 1,200 square metre garden will probably plant a number of fruit trees, placed carefully around the garden to be blossom features and to add height, shade and screening. Those with a 1,200 to 2,000 square metre or more garden will probably opt for a definite orchard area.

CHOICE OF FRUIT

Typical fruit trees that can grow well along the Costas include the following. Naturally the success will depend on the quality of your soil, the microclimate of your plot, height above sea level and extent of shelter/exposure.

For a typical 1,000 square metre garden at 300 metres (1,000 feet) our first choice would be - lemon, orange, tangerine, apricot, pear, nectarine, peach, plum, almond.

TYPICAL TREES THAT CAN DO WELL

FRUIT TREE	BELOW 100M	ABOVE 100M	ABOVE 400M
Orange	Yes	Yes	No
Lemon	Yes	Yes	No
Grapefruit	Yes	Yes	No
Peach	Yes	Yes	No
Nectarine	Yes	Yes	No
Paraguayo	Yes	?	No
Plum	Yes	Yes	?
Pear	Yes	Yes	?
Apple	?	Yes	Yes
Cherry	Yes	Yes	?
Níspero	Yes	Yes	?
Quince	Yes	Yes	?
Mulberry	Yes	Yes	?
Fig	Yes	Yes	Yes
Strawberry Tree	?	Yes	?
Persicum	Yes	Yes	?
Avocado	Yes	Yes	?
Grapevine	Yes	Yes	Yes
Banana	Yes	?	No
Exotics e.g. mango	Yes	?	No
Walnut	?	Yes	Yes
Almond	Yes	Yes	Yes

Yes = Good chance of success.
? = Depends on position.   No = Success doubtful.

PURCHASING TREES

1. Search out a reliable supplier. Ask neighbours and local orchard owners.
2. Look out for strong well-shaped young trees. Watch out for virus-free stock or disease-resistant stock.
3. If you are limited for space, ask for trees grown on dwarfing rootstocks.
4. Above all recognise that locally proven varieties are likely to be more successful and problem free than newly imported varieties

PLANTING

As most fruit trees are supplied with their roots restricted in a small pot of plastic sleeve or bare rooted (i.e. with no soil), special care needs to be given to planting.

The following broad guidelines are offered.
1. The autumn is the best time for planting.
2. Recognise that most mature fruit trees will grow to a diameter of four to five metres.
3. Dig a hole a metre deep and wide for planting.
4. Fill the hole with water and let the water drain away. Repeat. Spread the roots out evenly as a circular fan before infilling. Ensure any graft is above the level of the soil. Incorporate well-rotted compost, manure or bone meal in the planting soil.
5. Stake the tree carefully with a two-metre stake knocked half a metre into the soil. Tie the tree to the stake with a special plastic strap or wire threaded through a short length of old hosepipe.
6. Create a two-metre circumference watering moat with a half metre central pile around the trunk. Watering will then encourage outward root growth.
7. Water to keep the soil moist until established.

ONGOING CARE

1. Water most trees in the spring and summer to encourage the swelling of fruit buds and fruit. Figs, almonds, pomegranates and walnuts for instance will need little water when established. Fertilise fruit trees in the early spring and water in well. A circle of well-rotted manure fertilises, improves the soil structure/drainage through worm action and retains moisture. Excess fertiliser will stimulate leaf growth at the expense of fruiting.
2. When you water, flood rather than drip feed.
3. Most fruit trees are pruned as follows: -
a. prune out inward-growing branches to allow airflow and sunlight into the centre of the tree.
b. prune side shoots to encourage fruit buds.
c. prune out crossing crowding branches.
d. reduce long branches to encourage fruiting fans and maintain a good shape.
4. The only other work involved will be winter and spring sprays to prevent or cope with insects or disease.

Hopefully within a few years you will be picking basketfuls of fruit. But remember fruit trees take time to mature. Avocados may take more than 10 years to fruit. One of ours took more than 12 years to flower.

71. Establishing a soft fruit patch

Living in Spain, we can buy strawberries from February until July. However, many are forced by vast quantities of water and piped fertiliser.

Why not therefore, start your own patch of home-grown natural strawberries. And, if you live at 300 metres or above, why not add a row or two of tasty raspberries to shelter the strawberries from the wind. Redcurrants, blackcurrants and blackberries can also be grown.

SIZE OF PLOT

The following guidelines will help you calculate the size of plot required.
- A small plot of 20 strawberry plants, enough for two persons, will need 1.5- 2 square metres.
- 30 raspberry canes will need 7.5 - 10 square metres.
- Redcurrants and blackcurrants, a square metre each.

SITING OF PLOT

Soft fruit will grow best in a well-drained soil containing plenty of humus in a sunny position.

PREPARING THE GROUND

Prepare the ground during September for October or November planting. First, clear the chosen plot of perennial roots such as couch grass, docks, nettles etc. Make sure that you remove the roots. Second, dig the soil to the full length of a spade and incorporating plenty of moisture holding compost or manure. Also, spread an inch or two on the surface.

OBTAINING PLANTS

Watch out for plants in garden centres and the more traditional inland markets. With strawberries, look out for healthy-looking plants free of leaves that look diseased. Look out for pots that can be divided. With care, you may be able to plant out four small plants from each pot purchased. Friends might also be able to offer you runners from their established plants.

Raspberry canes are normally sold in bundles. Check that the roots are not totally dried out and that leaves are not evident as a result of being kept in a hot greenhouse or shop. It may pay you to go inland to higher, cooler nurseries.

Redcurrants and blackcurrants will be in pots or plastic bags. Look out for potentially strong plants with plenty of buds.

Strawberries can also be raised from seed. Plant seeds in pots from July to September. Seedlings should be strong enough to plant out by February or March.

PLANTING OUT

With all the soft fruits dig a hole, fill it with water and let it drain away before planting. Then plant ensuring that roots are spread out. Return the soil and firm, making sure that the soil level is below the lowest strawberry leaves and below the previous pruning line of other plants.

MULCHING

All soft fruits appreciate a good layer of compost or manure around them. This reduces moisture evaporation, smothers weeds and attracts soil enriching worms.

In our dry climate, it is also worth planting strawberries in holes in black plastic. Ensure that there is always 10 centimetres of mulch around raspberries, blackcurrants and redcurrants.

WATERING

Water well after planting and every week until the plants are established. They should then look after themselves during the winter with occasional watering. In the spring, water every week during the flowering and fruiting season.

FORCING

For early strawberries, cover in January with a cane framework and clear plastic. This will maintain the warm damp microclimate for early flowering and fruiting. But don't leave the plastic on during the hot months of July and August, to prevent the burning up of plants.

SLUGS

If the plastic is weighted down this will also help prevent snails and slugs from entering. If you see any, remove immediately. As a prevention, surround the plot with a line of sharp sand, pine needles or comfrey leaves.

BASIC PLANT CARE

1. Remove dead leaves as they occur.
2. Remove and pot-up strong strawberry runners.
3. Cut out dead raspberry canes after each year's fruiting.
4. When raspberry canes grow to a metre, tie them to a wire attached to posts at either end of the line. They can grow to two metres and will then need a second support wire.
5. Each winter, prune redcurrant and blackcurrant bushes to shape.
6. Trim back blackberry bushes to shape, to stimulate fruiting spurs.

BLACKBERRIES

If you like blackberries, there are two possibilities. Pick them from the many wild bushes in the inland valleys or plant your own bushes in an out of the way corner of the garden. They need space to spread and don't really fit into the soft fruit plot. It is possible to train them along wires but to do this you will need to keep them well pruned.

72. Grapevines

We consider the selection, planting, ongoing pruning, watering, feeding and pest control required. In preparing the guidelines we took into account the small garden with a single vine as well as the large garden with a sizeable vineyard.

SELECTION OF VINES

Variety	Main Use			
	Eating	Mosto/Juice	Wine	Raisins
Aledo	--	■	---	---
Moscatel	■	■	White	■
Saltanina	■	---	---	---
Cardinal	■	---	---	---
Sylvanar	---	■	White	---
Macabeo	---	■	White	---
Mesequera	---	■	White	---
Cabernet Suavignon	---	■	Red	---
Merlot	---	■	Red	---
Monastrell	---	■	Red	---
Tempranillo	---	■	Red	---

The above are among the popular Mediterranean vines grown. Whatever variety you choose, select vines which are dormant or just starting to shoot in February/March. Vines with a strong trunk and root system. One-year cuttings will take three or four years to produce heavy crops. Potted up mature vines will be quicker to fruit provided they were dug up and potted carefully.

PLANTING VINES

Vines are best planted from November to February. Vines can grow in any soil including very arid and impoverished soil provided that it is well drained. Measure the spread of the root system. Dig a hole twice the spread and 50cm deep. Break up the hard earth pan at the bottom of the hole. Line the bottom of the hole with fragments of broken earthenware pots or stones. Vines need a speedy drainage of storm water. Line the hole with 10cm of well-rotted compost or manure. Cover this with 5cms of a good well draining planting mix. We suggest a mix of the removed garden soil, well-rotted manure, wood ash and coarse grit.

If vines have been purchased with dry roots, soak the roots in a bucket of water for an hour. Then place the vine in the hole, spreading the roots as wide as possible. Fill the hole with the planting mix, firm, mulch and water well. Commercial vines are normally planted with two metres between vines and with two metres between rows. Cordon wires are normally 50 or 100cm above the ground.

PRUNING

a. After planting
New vines need an early pruning. But first decide on the format you plan to train them to. There are three possibilities.

FORMAT	USE
Bush	Vineyards
Standards	Vineyards on wires, and garden over pergolas to provide summer shade.
Cordons	Vineyards on wires, and gardens against sunny walls.

Cut all back to four buds and allow the plant to grow freely for a year before starting to train.

b. Pruning at end of first year
- Prune in February or March, after the risk of frost.

Bush or standards - cut back each of the four branches that have grown to four eyes.
Cordons - train the strongest branch along a wire fixed between posts or along a wall.
- cut back to a metre and reduce to four buds, the fourth being below the branch to make it easier to tie up later growth.
- cut off the weaker branches. Seal cuts

c. Second and third winter.
As for the first winter prune in February or March.
Bush or standards - cut back to four fruiting eyes on each of the four main branches that are now thickening up. Seal ends.
Cordons - cut main branches trained on wires back to eight buds. Seal ends.

d. Summer pruning
Cut out all shoots below the fruiting branches. Cut out any weak leaders. Cut out any non-flowering shoots. When flowers are formed pinch out tips of fruiting laterals.
Main branches on all types can be allowed to grow four or five metres. Don't cut these too hard, only to keep scraggily tidy. The leaves are critical for the generation of internal nutrients by photosynthesis.

WATERING

Vines require little water except at three stages of their growth - when first planted to stimulate root growth, just before flowering time to help formation, and when ripening to swell fruit.

FEEDING AND PROTECTION

Vines need little feeding. However they will respond to a light spring mulch of well-rotted manure or compost, but not too much or too rich.

Vines suffer most under humid conditions. As a precaution shake sulphur very early morning over the entire vine from February onwards, more frequently if a problem occurs. Put the sulphur in a sock and shake to give a fine covering. We suggest you use a mask.

Continue to treat when grapes are at the final fattening stage or changing colour from green to red or black. But use much less, a puffer would be a good idea, and don't do it in the hot sun.

If it rains when the grapes are ripening spray lightly with copper sulphate, to treat fungi that can develop.

If the above doesn't work for you, ask for a specialist proprietary spray at your local agricultural co-operative.

HARVESTING GRAPES

Grapes will be ready for picking between early August and the end of September depending on the variety, exposure to sun and altitude. The longer the grapes are left, the sweeter they will become and the acidity goes down.

73. Citrus trees

No garden on the Costas is complete without one or two citrus trees, provided you have the water to water them.

Oranges, lemons and grapefruits are an essential part of the ambience of the climate, traditions and cuisine of the Mediterranean coast. What can be better than fresh orange or grapefruit juice from the garden for breakfast, and a fresh lemon for cooking or the evening gin and tonic? In many parts of the Costas, particularly the Valencia region, citrus fruits are grown in abundance commercially. One might conclude that they are easy trees to grow, but they are not. They need much loving care to produce strong trees that will fruit well for 25 years or more.

We therefore consider the benefits and choice of citrus trees, their planting and aftercare. Included are some of the tips we have learnt from some of the professional growers. We find they work in our garden.

1. BENEFITS OF CITRUS TREES

- Your own fruit most of the year.
- The perfume of the blossom.
- Evergreens that grow into majestic mature trees.
- Colourful trees with ripening fruit.
- Can be grown as isolated trees, orchards or hedges.

2. CHOICE OF CITRUS FRUITS

You will find a wide range of varieties and cultivars available in nurseries. Some popular varieties are listed below.

Fruit	Popular variety	Typical harvest time
Lemon	Luna	All year round
	Lisbon	November-May
Orange (sweet)	Navel	October-February
	Valencia Late	January-May
	Berna	March-June
Orange (sour)	Seville	December-March
Mandarin	Salzara	November-February
Satsuma	Miyagawa	October-January
Clementine/Tangerine	Oroval	November-January
Grapefruit	Star Ruby	November-March
Kumquat	Fortunella	November-March

Decide whether you want mature already fruiting trees or are happy to wait for young plants to mature naturally. Recognise that citrus trees can become large trees over 20 or 30 years. Commercially they are cut for firewood and replaced at 20/25 years. Citrus logs are excellent for burning.

There are two main problems with growing citrus fruits. Firstly diseases and secondly drought resistance. Plant breeders are continually producing new cultivars, so seek out disease and drought resistant varieties. Explain to the garden centre where you plan to plant, i.e. where you live, the type of soil and water and whether you are going to plant in the garden or in pots.

Lime will grow in sheltered places.

3. FORMATS

Citrus fruits can be pruned and trained as bushes, trees and cordons. It is also possible to graft several varieties onto one tree. But that's fun for the future!

4. PLANTING

- In theory container grown plants can be planted at any time of year. However January to March is normally best. During winter months they can be caught by cold winds before they are acclimatised to the microclimate in your garden.
- Dig a planting hole as deep as the root ball and twice its diameter. Citrus trees are normally supplied in especially deep containers. Keep dug soil for filling the hole.
- Carefully remove the tree from its container. Cut it out rather than pulling so as not to damage any roots or loosen the soil around the root ball.
- Ensure you plant the stem at the same or slightly higher height than in the nursery. Soil above the original soil line causes ideal conditions for disease.
- Infill with the soil you dug out. Don't mix in manure or compost. If you do the tree could sink below the planting line thus encouraging trunk rot.
- Rake out a basin around the planted tree and water thoroughly.

5. WATERING

- Water young trees regularly for the first few years after planting and then when dry.
- Water at the drip line to encourage root growth.
- Give all trees a good soaking in the month before and during flowering when the fruits are setting. Also a month before ripening.
- Alternate watering and drying allows oxygen to enter the soil, which is beneficial.
- Ensure that excess water can drain away Citrus fruits do not like to be water logged.
- Citrus trees in pots need constant care.

6. FEEDING

- Citrus trees dislike fertiliser or well-rotted manure in the planting hole, the roots are delicate and can be easily burnt.

- Delay feeding via a liquid feed or organic mulch until the autumn after planting and then feed only sparingly.
- Mulches are very beneficial both as a feed and for reducing evaporation, but keep away from the trunk to prevent diseases.
- The main feeding should be in January/February. Spread the manure or sprinkle the proprietary feed around the drip line of the tree.

7. SPRAYING

- Citrus trees can attract a number of diseases including the "minero" plague of recent years recognised by the curling of leaves. We originally used chemical sprays, but now use neem, an extract from the nim tree which is an organic pesticide.
- Spray in February/March and October/November or when the problems appear.

8. WEEDING

- Dig in weeds, especially the colourful spring clover that spreads from orchards to gardens from January to April. Dig it in before it dies back in April to provide valuable nitrogen to the roots.
- Generally keep the well around the trees weed free.

9. PRUNING

In general citrus trees need little pruning.

- Remove trunk suckers below the grafting union.
- Within the garden the appearance is often as important as fruit yield, but restrict pruning of young trees to shortening out-of-shape vigorous growth. In time a citrus tree will find its own full shape.
- Unless you want to train a tree so that you can walk under it, leave the lower branches to maximise the yield of fruit.
- If the emergent crop is heavy after flowering, remove the centre growth of the three shoots at the end of fruiting branches. This keeps the tree open and creates strong fruiting branches.
- Thin fruits as they swell to produce larger fruits - but less of course.
- Lemons are the exception in pruning. They tend to grow in a more vigorous upright manner than oranges. Therefore prune to shape and keep the tree low enough to pick lemons easily.
- Trees in poor shape, even old trees, can often be rejuvenated by cutting back all branches heavily towards the stem in February or March. Seal all cuts with a pruning compound

We hope that these basic guidelines help you to develop healthy trees and substantial crops. A friend, Manolo, has a 20-year-old tree that yields up to 600 kilos of lemons annually! Its mature roots found the exit from the sceptic tank years ago!

74. *Cash crop trees*

Cash crop trees can be useful inheritances or additions to the garden. There are several possibilities.

Firstly, if you have mature trees such as carob, almond, olive, walnut, avocado or plum, the possibilities are obvious. The income may not be great but they will make a contribution to garden expenses.

Carob beans are often seen as a dirty nuisance. Many people cut mature trees down even though they are one of the best trees for shade. Yet, there are buyers of carob beans in many villages. There is an increasing demand from the health food and paint industries. Knock the ripe black pods off the trees during August/early September. A long cane will speed up the process. Bag the pods, preferably in hessian sacks. Most buyers will supply them on request. It is preferable not to bag up in plastic bags as the pods will sweat and rot. With luck, the pods from a large tree will pay for next year's seeds and plants, and you would have had to clear up the mess anyway!

If you have 20 or more olive trees you may be able to sell the olives to the local olive mill or find a villager who will pick your crop, sharing some with you in exchange for pruning your trees annually. You will have better-looking flowering trees and the villager will have a better crop. If you only have one or two trees then pick your own olives between November and January, depending on type and location. There will not be sufficient to sell but it is a relatively easy task to pickle your own olives. Once tasted you won't want to eat tinned ones again.

Like olive trees, almonds and walnut trees need careful pruning to stimulate good crops of large nuts. These you will probably be able to sell into local greengrocers. Small nuts you won't. Again, use them yourself for cooking and snacks. They will be fresher and taste better than many from the supermarket. Both will store in a dry cellar for a couple of years without deterioration.

Good sized avocados, plums and other fruit will be saleable or tradable with friends. With village shops, you will probably find much local competition.

If you are lucky, you will have inherited one or two pine nut producing pine trees. When the large, round cones, much like a globe artichoke, fall they should be dried in the sun and then stored. As you need pine kernels, shake them out of the cones and de-shell. You will have a constant supply of fresh pine kernels for cooking, especially for the centre of paella meatballs. To be able to sell them you would need a sizeable copse of trees. You will see them on the outskirts of villages as you drive round. If you have not inherited cash crop trees, then recognise that planting an orchard or plantation will be a major task, without an immediate return, except increased privacy and the spring blossom display. A neighbour of ours planted a small field of 50 olive trees as an inheritance for his three-year-old grandchild. Spanish families still plant trees as one used to lay down port!

75. Pruning of fruit trees

All fruit trees need some pruning annually. But some more than others. We provide some general guidelines. They are based on our experience over the years, what we have learnt from elderly Spaniards, for whom pruning is an inherited art, and the debate between heavy pruners and ecological fruit growers who minimise pruning.

WHY PRUNE?

There are a number of reasons for pruning fruit trees.
1. To stimulate flowering side shoots and fruit buds.
2. To divert rising sap from excess foliage to swelling fruit.
3. To improve the quantity of fruit by stimulating the growth of fruiting side shoots for next year.
4. To improve the size of the fruit.
5. To improve the shape and appearance of the tree as a feature or to hide the house next door or to give shade.
6. To allow ventilation between branches and around ripening fruit by cutting out crossing laterals.
7. To let the sun shine on ripening fruit by cutting out the centre.
8. To create space between trees.
9. To create special formats such as cordons, espaliers and pyramids.
10. To reduce the height of fruiting branches to make picking possible from the ground.
11. To prevent long branches breaking from the overload of heavy crops or from storms.
12. To reduce the stress on the root system. Fruit trees will grow larger in good soil.
13. To improve garden hygiene by cutting out or pruning dead, diseased or pest covered branches.

WHY REDUCE THE EXTENT OF TRADITIONAL PRUNING?

1. Over pruning upsets the balance of the tree between growth stimulants from the air by photosynthesis in the leaves and growth stimulants from the soil via the roots.
2. Well prepared and planted trees find there own natural form and adapt to variations in microclimate. Good crops one year and not the next are normally the effect of nature not pruning .
3. Poor pruning can allow diseases to enter. There therefore needs to be a balance in planning your pruning,

WHAT FORMAT TO PURCHASE OR PRUNE TO?

- Fruit trees can be trained in nine main formats. Normally bastion, standard, bush, cordon, espalier, umbrella, pyramid, fan and wine glass or 'U'.

A well pruned olive

- Most fruit trees are pruned to create standard, bush or pyramid forms. The bastion form can be useful in small gardens.
- Cordons and espaliers can be trained along wires attached to posts to create a screen within the garden - perhaps between the flower and vegetable garden.
- Cordons, espaliers, fans and 'U's can be trained on wires or rings fixed to a house or garden wall. These formats are particularly useful for peaches, pears, plums and nectarines.
- The umbrella format can be formed by training a standard tree that has long branches naturally, such as cherry, over a wire frame attached to three-metre posts. This can create a pleasant shady arbor for outdoor eating.
- It is also possible to purchase fruit trees such as apple, pear, peach and plum on regular, semi-dwarf or dwarf root stocks. The many choices of formats and heights provide plenty of scope for integrating fruit trees into both small and large gardens.

WHEN TO PRUNE?

a. Winter pruning.
The main pruning should be done during the winter months when a tree is dormant or when the sap is just starting to rise. This is when buds start to show signs of swelling.
Ensure that all major cuts are sealed with a pruning sealant or lump of mud to prevent disease from entering.
b. Summer pruning.
Restrict summer pruning to keeping an ornamental tree in shape, thinning heavy crops and shortening side shoots to stimulate buds for next year.

WHAT TO PRUNE WITH?

The following are the best tools to use
a. A curved pruning saw.
b. Secateurs.
c. Extendable pruning shears.
d. A step ladder - trees can be dangerous when climbed into.

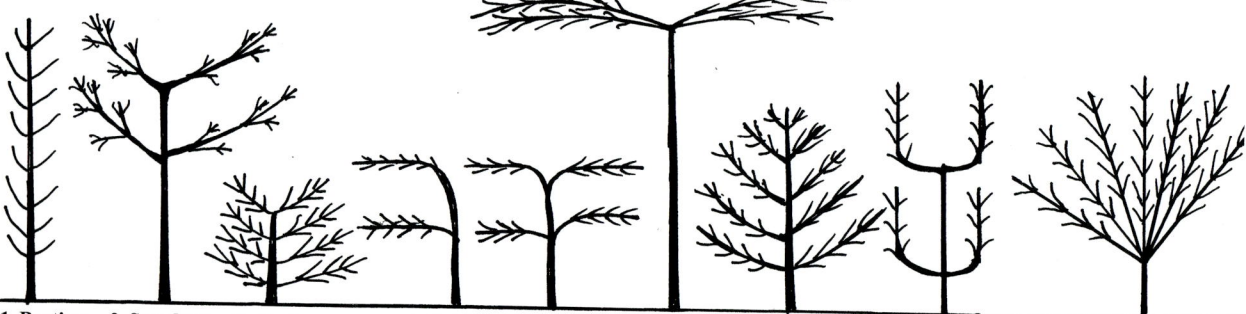

1. Bastion   2. Standard   3. Bush   4. Cordon   5. Espalier   6. Umbrella   7. Pyramid   8. Wine Glass   9. Fan

e. One sees Spaniards using an axe aimed accurately with every stroke. We regard this as too dangerous for the amateur gardener.

HOW TO PRUNE?

Do little pruning on young trees for the first three or four years until the root system is established.

TYPE OF FORMAT:

STANDARD, UMBRELLA OR BUSH, e.g. cherry, apricot and plum
Cut out central vertical branches and criss crossing laterals to open up the centre.
When too long cut back main branches by one third of their length.
Cut back budding side shoots to just above a flower bud.
Reduce non-flowering side shoots by half or remove if overcrowded.

BASTION OR PYRAMID, e.g. quince, nectarine, pear and pomegranate
Cut back the main trunk when the required height, say two metres, is reached to stimulate lateral side branches.

CORDONS, ESPALIER AND 'U's, e.g. peach, nectarine and pear
Retain two or four branches and train onto wires or wall ties.
Reduce lengths as required.
Reduce fruiting side shoots to two or three fruiting buds.

CAROB TREES
These were traditionally shaped as a wide vertical column. The height and width being equal. The effect can be attractive.

OLIVE TREES
Prune a month after harvesting the olives.
Young trees can be pruned to create a basic framework of one, two, three or four trunks growing up from the thick base trunk just above ground level. In general, the more trunks, the more olives.
The height of an olive tree can be reduced to make harvesting easier by training low growing branches outwards.
When fruiting branches become long and straggly cut back the main branches to a half or even a third of their length. Olive trees soon sprout out again and good crops will be achieved the second year.
Olive trees can survive for several centuries. Left unpruned they can grow into majestic trees up to 15 or more metres in height.
Summer prune to reduce the number of fruiting branches to stimulate large olives.

FIG TREES
As other fruits, but as with olives, mature trees can be rejuvenated by cutting main branches back by half or even two thirds of their length.

ALMOND TREES
Cut out unnecessary main branches to create a well shaped tree with an open centre in December.
Prune out non-fruiting shoots as buds begin to swell in January.

76. *Natural feeds and sprays*

Many natural or organic feeds, insecticides and fungicide sprays are available. Useful to both the flower and vegetable gardener. We have referred to them in many chapters. Our advice is collated in this chapter for convenience. The natural feeds and sprays we use regularly are summarised below.

METHODS OF PREPARATION

1. An infusion - Pour boiling water over fresh or dried ingredients. Leave to stand for 10 minutes and strain. Used for preparing extractions from leaves and non-woody stems, e.g. nettle and tomato leaves.

2. A decoction - Bring herbs and plants to the boil and simmer for 15 minutes. Used for extracting the beneficial properties out of the stems of plants and bulbs, e.g. horsetail and garlic.

3. Decomposition - Leave leaves to rot naturally with or without water in a large plastic barrel, e.g. comfrey leaves.

In each case it is preferable to use non-chlorinated water, especially for potassium soap sprays.

A. NATURAL FEEDS

FEED	PREPARE BY	TYPICAL USES
Comfrey - source of potash	Decomposition of leaves without water added or with water.	Dilute 40:1 when decomposed without water or 20:1 with water added. Stimulates extraction of essential trace elements from the soil.
Manure	Decomposition in water.	Liquid feed for young and maturing plants.
Nettles - source of nitrogen	Decomposition in water 1kg fresh leaves in 10 litres of water 200g dried leaves in 10 litres of water	Feed to plants before flowering and fruiting to encourage strong growth. Dilute 10:1 Especially beneficial to green leaved vegetables Spray feed to strengthen young and sickly plants. Dilute 20:1.
Cocktail of above three	Equal parts of diluted comfrey manure and nettle.	A powerful mix to develop strong plants.

B. NATURAL SPRAYS

FEED	PREPARE BY	TYPICAL USES
Horses' Tail	100g fresh stems without roots to 1.5litre water or 25g dried herbs to 1.5litre water	A general spray against fungal diseases. Spray plants and soil. Also useful for leaf curl.
Garlic	Decoction 2 crushed whole bulbs to 1 litre water	Spray against aphids and beetles and geranium moth.
Tomato Leaves	Infusion - handful of leaves to 1 litre water	Spray against rust on roses and vegetables
Potassium soap	Decoction - Dilute 50g per litre of water.	Dilute 10:1. Spray against aphids.

The above is not gardening witchcraft. We have merely resurrected old village practices. The benefits are not only those summarised in the table above. Most importantly, natural feeds and sprays:-

1. Protect beneficial insects and animals - especially worms.
2. Reduce:-
 - the potential hazards from using strong chemicals.
 - residual concentration on the skin of fruit and vegetables.
 - personal dangers when using.
 - storage and spillages especially where children and pets are resident.
 - chemical smells in the garage, shed or greenhouse.

Proprietary ecological insecticides are increasingly available. Particularly useful is neem, an extract from the East Asian nim tree. It is widely used to protect mining insects on citrus, peach and nectarine trees. It can also be used to keep away aphids, etc. on the vegetable plot, without harming the beneficial insects etc.

77. Waterless gardening

Along the Costas, water is a valuable commodity, especially for gardens. In recent years we appear to have been in a cycle of drier years with longer periods of drought and low rainfalls when it occurs. Some years ago, local and national water storage levels lead to restrictions and bans on the use of hose pipes and piped watering systems.

We therefore consider it important to reduce the demand for water in our gardens and move to what we term "Waterless Gardening" (WG). We define WG as the art of minimising the need for water and getting just sufficient water to the roots of plants Not only for reasons of cost or shortage but also to reduce the long term impact of residual chemicals from chlorinated town water and high nitrate agricultural water on tender plants and trees. So what practical actions can we take? The following are suggested for the typical flower and shrub garden.

1. Plant plants that do not require much water once established. Plant more deep rooted perennials, shrubs and corms and cut back on the ever thirsty annuals. Good choices include succulents, herbs such as rosemary and thyme. Lilies, lantanas, yuccas, cacti, palms, gazanias, echiums, plumbago, oleander etc.

2. Ensure that new plants are planted in humus-rich soil. Gradually enrich the soil in all beds by digging in compost in the autumn and by regular mulching.

3. Make your major plantings in the autumn to allow roots to start to grow deep during the winter. Do not plant new plants after the end of April.

4. Plant plants through sheets of perforated black plastic and cover with peat substitute, compost, gravel or attractive stone chippings. This helps reduce evaporation and keeps roots cool. You can also plant shrubs through newspaper and mulch with grass cuttings.

5. Keep plants in plant pots in the shade They can easily be moved out into the sun to brighten up sunny areas for the barbecue party etc. Paint or varnish the inside of terracotta pots to prevent continuous evaporation. Water potted plants by standing in a tray of water rather than watering from the top. This will encourage roots to grow down rather than up and reduce the number of root bound potted plants.

6. Plant plants closer together in groups and increase the areas covered by ground cover plants such as the grey leaved gazanias, low growing purple lantanas and lavender. Again they will reduce water evaporation, soil cracking and provide natural shade for roots.

7. If you have to water, then water late evening or during the night to reduce evaporation loss. Water away from plant stems and tree trunks to stimulate a wider root system. If you have a drip watering system check regularly for leaks and that all sprays/drip heads are distributing water usefully. Remove redundant drip/spray heads.

8. Use cool washing up water in a watering can for less tender plants. Consider diverting sink and bath water to a holding tank and feed flower/shrub beds by gravity.

9. Increase the areas of path and terrace. Stone chippings laid over plastic sheet are attractive, quick to lay and less expensive than concreted stone slabs or tiles, also the design and layout of stone chipping paths and terraces can be easily adjusted until you are satisfied with the effect. Several times in a month if necessary.

10. Reduce the lawn area or don't have a lawn at all. This does not mean a concrete desert but a network of well-placed terraces and paths with large areas of plants and shrubs. Visit a few old Spanish palaces in Andulacia with large gardens. Few have lawns.

We hope that these 10 ideas stimulate a reduction in the need for and the use of water in the garden. And at the same time lead to more colourful and interesting gardens.

78. *Maximising water retention*

Maximising the retention of any rain water from a shower or storm is critical on the Costas. We look at 21 ways of achieving this in a practical manner.

1. Install guttering along the edge of all or some roofs and collect storm water in a 'deposito' or barrel.

2. If you don't like the idea of guttering construct main shrub beds below the eves. These will be less damaged than annual biennials by cascading rain water. Mulch shrubs, cover the mulch with black plastic and cover the plastic with attractive stone chippings.

3. Construct all paths and terraces so that water runs off to water flower beds.

4. Construct the slopes within the garden and internal and boundary walls so that rainwater is fed to where required.

5. Build a low wall around all boundaries to prevent the loss of water over boundaries.

6. Slope the end of the driveway so that water runs back into the garden and is not lost through the gateway to the road. Why give away valuable water!

7. Increase the ratio of paths and terraces to planted areas to more than 50 per cent. If you construct paths with draining material such as stone chippings lay these on plastic sheeting. The water will flow sideways to feed adjacent plants. The water table under the plastic will not evaporate or feed weeds.

8. Channel surplus water from paths or terrace to :

a. Top up the pond.

b. The vegetable plot.

9. Surround the pond with rocks, perhaps even a large rockery with plants planted between touching rocks.

10. Plant shrubs close so that mature plants overlap and create continuous shade for roots. Leave a layer of rotting leaves under shrubs. They create a natural compost mulch. They don't have to look untidy.

11. Plant most vegetables through holes in black plastic sheeting. Also drip feed using large plastic water bottles with drip nozzles fitted through the side.

12. Continually mulch vegetables and soft fruit with well-rotted manure, compost or grass cuttings. They retain water and repress weeds.

13. Collect newspapers. Make a dilute mix of water and wallpaper paste. Soak newspapers overnight in the mix, in a large container in the garden. Use to create a multi layer - about half centimetre thick - around roses and shrubs. Cover with a shallow layer of earth or grass cuttings.

14. Run excess water from selected paths or terraces into underground depositos from which water can be brought by gravity or a pond pump to areas of the garden between rains.

15. Mulch the top layer of window boxes with a thick layer of moss or a centimetre slice of sponge.

16. Use ground cover plants to cover all soil areas.

17. Maximise the use of small rocks or pebbles laid on plastic with holes in it for your plants to prevent water evaporation. Well weathered stones look more attractive than riverbed pebbles.

18. Plant more trees to increase the area of shade and semishade. Select trees that require little water.

19. Minimise the area of lawn. Lawns are high users of water.

20. Increase the surface area covered by paths and terraces. Water will be retained so plant alongside so that roots seek out the damper and cooler soil.

21. Use water crystals in pots. They absorb water and release it to the roots at a controlled rate.

79. Installation and improvement of watering systems

No two gardens are the same but for all, watering is one of the greatest gardening problems on the Costas. We would all like to water our plants regularly without restriction. However, this is not possible for most. We should accept the problem of water and try to create gardens that do not require continuous heavy watering. We need to grow more plants that withstand the long, hot Spanish summers.

The best solution is to grow more of what the Spanish grow - bougainvilleas, hibiscus, lantanas, plumbagos, palms, cacti, begonias, margaritas, gazanias etc. There are so many to choose from. Nevertheless, when first planted they do need water until they establish strong, deep root systems. Watering with a hose wastes water. If the ground is dry it just runs away. If you dig a ring of earth around your plant it will help but this surface watering often stimulates the roots of the plants to grow upwards rather than downwards, thus reducing their drought resistance. A better solution is therefore a drip watering system. However, for success this needs to be carefully thought out. The best time for working on a watering system is when new shrubs and plants have just been planted, or when plants are dormant and just pruned back in the winter.

The following guidelines are suggested:

1. Draw up a sketch of your garden.

2. Mark those plants that need regular water and those that do not. The latter include mature plants, cacti and succulents.

3. Mark your source of water.

4. Mark up the best route or possible routes for main supply pipes.

5. Decide whether it would be more efficient to have -
- One main supply tube from which side tubes feed water to specific plants - all plants being watered at the same time and to the same extent.
- A number of sub-systems feeding water to various zones of the garden and then to individual plants. In this case the system could be adjusted to feed water at different rates to different areas and at different times by the use of hand valves and a computer control system.

6. Decide whether you need a simple battery run time clock attached to the main supply or a more complex multi-zone control system. In this case it would need to be connected to a mains electricity supply. Both will enable you to water at night, at specific times, for specific periods i.e. every 48 hours at 04.00 for 30 minutes.

7. Decide on the size of the main tubing you require. Our experience is that 1.5cm tubing is better than 1cm tubing. It blocks up less frequently from calcium deposits and earth. From experience, locating and clearing blockages in small tubes can be a very time consuming and frustrating task.

8. Decide on the size of the side tubing to use to feed individual plants. Also whether to use drip or spray heads. We prefer the former. They are easy to adjust and do not lose much water by evaporation.

9. Decide where best to join side tubes to the main tubes. Buy main tubing without pre-made holes. This allows you total flexibility. Easy-to-use kits are available including a hole puncher, drip heads, plugs etc.

10. Decide where small turn-off valves would be useful. Initially you may want to feed some recently planted shrubs or trees frequently. But once established you might only water under severe drought conditions. You might also need to water a bed of annuals throughout the summer but not in the autumn when flowering has finished.

11. Now order the materials and build up the system.

12. Test the system by turning the supply on full and looking for leaks.

13. Deal with the leaks and then balance the system by checking and adjusting the water flow from each drip feed.

14. Set up your timing system and leave to operate. Our experience is that it is better to provide the roots of plants with a good soaking only every few days rather than a short period of shallow watering for a few minutes a day. We suggest you start with 30 minutes every 48 hours. Check the moisture around plants each day and adjust the supply to keep the soil just moist. Naturally in wet periods the system can be turned off. If there is week after week of drought, the time of watering can be increased.

15. Do not open up the mains tap that feeds system more than half. Maximum pressure will blow joints. Strengthen joints by jubilee clips.

16. Once the system is operating make a monthly inspection tour of the system.
- Check each joint. Watch for leaks
- Check drips - that they drip, are not blocked and that they are firmly connected to the main tubes.
- Check that there is a feed to all-important plants. Extend the system if necessary.
- Check that feeds are not now redundant - block off as necessary.
- If you have a multi-zone timing system, check that all the zones come on in the sequence planned and that the supply times are all still appropriate to the time of year and weather conditions.

17. Recognise that it is expensive, unnecessary and socially irresponsible to use the watering system during all weeks of the year. Only use it when establishing new plants and when helping mature plants survive drought conditions.

Spanish plants are well able to adapt to dry conditions. Indeed, many plants go dormant during the second half of July and August. Once the weather cools off at the end of September/early October most plants come back to life. The best gardens have a good display of colour during November and December and March to July.

80. *Adding a garden frame or greenhouse*

The addition of a garden frame and a greenhouse to the garden can be very beneficial to the enthusiastic gardener even on the hot Costas. With our climate you may ask why!

1. THE BENEFITS

A. The Garden Frame
a. The propagation of a wide range of plants for the flower garden from cuttings.
b. The raising of annual and perennial plants including shrubs from seeds.
c. The growing of early varieties of vegetables, e.g. melons, cucumbers, lettuces and radishes.
d. Sheltering pots of delicate cacti or alpines from winter rains or frosts in the inland valleys.

B. The Greenhouse
As the garden frame plus
a. Growing a collection of cacti, succulents, alpines or exotic bulbs.
b. Growing tall plantlets until the plants and the soil are ready for planting out.
c. Forcing an early grapevine.
d. Growing of early tomatoes and cucumbers in pots or in the ground.
e. Storage for garden tools.

The above benefits may well stimulate you to construct one or both this autumn. We therefore look at some of the important issues involved.

2. SITING

In northern Europe we would probably have sited our garden frame and greenhouse in full sun to achieve the temperatures necessary to germinate and grow on seedlings. On the Costas, low temperatures will not normally be a problem. Rather the reverse. The most practical siting is therefore in semi shade in a position that avoids the midday sun. We have ours on the west side of a hedge and house respectively. The only direct sunlight is mid-afternoon onwards. They are conveniently warmed up until sunset, thus achieving a warm overnight microclimate.

3. GARDEN FRAME

Design
- The size of garden frame will depend on the number of boxes of seedlings or containers of cuttings you anticipate raising
- We suggest you start with a 1x1 or 2x1 metre frame. You can add units of the same size if you want to expand your raising of new plants.
- For a permanent frame it is worth building brick side walls. Wood can be used but is less durable. Wooden sides are however the best for portable frames.
- The covers are safer in plastic than glass. However, they need to be held down firmly by metal hooks and eyes or elastic ties over hooks.
- Shade with green woven material for hot days.
- Treat all woodwork with two coats of an ecological preservative.

Prevention of snails and disease
- Ensure that there are no gaps under the base of the side walls or between the covers and side walls that would allow snails to enter. A warm frame is ideal as winter shelter for them!
- Look around the frame every time you open it for signs of snails in case one or two have forced a way in.
- Wash seed and plant boxes, containers and pots with a dilute bleach solution followed by a clear rinse before filling with seed or potting compost. Empty the garden frame for a few hours once a year. Remove rubbish. Spray the sides and covers with an antifungal spray.

Keep plants moist
- The loss of plants is generally due to drying out or rotting from too much water. One has to find a happy mid point by trial and error.
- Ensure that the soil in containers is never allowed to dry. Aim to have it damp but not wet.
- To reduce the risk of young plants and cuttings rotting away add an ecological fungicide to all water used in a watering can or spray.
- Check that the soil in the base of the pots as well as the top are moist.
- Combine top watering with bottom watering in very hot weather

Hardening Off
- Remove the covers for a week during the day and then entirely. Or take pots out at this stage if other plants are staying in the frames.

4. THE GREENHOUSE

Design
- The greenhouse can be constructed for use solely as a greenhouse or as a combined greenhouse/garden tool shed.
- The minimum useful size is probably six cubic metres, as a lean-too against the house or garden wall.
- Roof and sides can be of glass or plastic. The latter is safer and is a better insulator. Also it will not get as hot.
- Roof and side ventilation will be essential.

Possible Special Features
- A built in propagator .
- A spray atomiser.
- Thermostatically controlled heating for the winter months.

The opportunities with a garden frame and greenhouse are endless. Why not start constructing one or both ready for next year's early plantings?

81. Garden safety

Garden safety is important to all home owners and gardeners. Gardens may be beautiful but they contain many hazards. We base the following check list on our own experience.

1. ELECTRICITY
Have you installed a separate trip for the garden circuit?
Are all outside circuits in heavy armoured cable?
Are all cables laid inside strong plastic conduits, buried 20 cm deep and covered with slabs or concrete in areas where spades or forks etc. may be used?
Are all fittings special waterproof fittings and undamaged?

2. CHEMICAL STORAGE
Are all garden chemicals kept in a secure place on high shelving away from pets and children or in secure bins?
Are the chemical containers all sound with secure tops and no leakages?
Are all chemicals clearly labelled?
Are all out of date chemicals put in the appropriate container at a local eco park?

3. GARDEN CLOTHING
Do we wear appropriate protective clothing when adding fertilisers, weedkilling or spraying? Do we have good quality protective hats, goggles, face masks, gloves and shoes?
Are they regularly cleaned and washed?
Is the sprayer well maintained? When it leaks is it immediately repaired or changed?
Do we wear shoes with tough tops when digging, raking, hoeing or cutting grass?
Do we always use garden knives away from us and not towards us?

4. USE OF ECOLOGICAL SOLUTIONS
Have we or should we change to less hazardous natural/organic/ecological fertilisers, herbicides and insecticides?
Have we identified and located reliable sources for each?
Have we started to grow plants that can be used as:
a. fertilisers (e.g. comfrey and nettles)
b. insecticides (e.g. garlic, lavender, rosemary, catmint)
c. fungicides (e.g. horsetail and nettles)
d. foliar feed (e.g. nettle)
e. beneficial insect attractors for pollination (e.g. rosemary, borage)
f. beneficial insect attractors to divert them from vegetables (e.g. coriander, nasturtiums and fennel)
g. beneficial insect repellents (e.g. chives, garlic, marigolds)

5. VEGETABLES AND FRUIT
Are all vegetables and fruit washed before cooking or eating raw?

6. TOOLS AND EQUIPMENT
Are all tools regularly cleaned?
Are loose/broken handles immediately tightened or repaired?
Are tools with sharp edges stored safely?
Are guards and safety catches on machines secure and used?
Are safety catches on secateurs operating correctly?

7. TOOL SHED
Is the tool shed kept tidy to reduce the chance of trips, cuts and spillages?

8. STINGING INSECTS
Are nests of wasps and hornets speedily identified and destroyed?

9. TREES
Are dead and dangerous branches cut down before they fall?
Are all trees securely stacked?

10. PRICKLY PLANTS
Are prickly plants sited and cut back to reduce the chance of accidents?
Are the spiky ends of yuccas cut off to reduce the chance of eye and head injuries?
Are strong gloves and thick clothing worn when pruning palms, yucca cacti, blackberries, etc.?
Have we reduced the number of prickly plants in the garden or even banned them?

11. POISONOUS PLANTS
Have we identified those plants that are poisonous, avoided them or planted them away from paths and warned the family and visitors? (e.g. datura, morning glory and oleander).

12. DANGEROUS POINTS
Do we ensure that the ends of canes or supporting posts are blunt to avoid eye injuries when leaning over plants?
Have we pruned back low branches on ornamental and fruit trees to the trunk and not left dangerous ends at head height?
Are the ends of wire ties tied in tightly and not left as dangerous snags?

13. GLASS
Do we use plastic rather than glass for cloches, garden frames and the greenhouse?

14. PATHS AND TERRACES
Are all paths and terraces well maintained and constructed from non-slip materials??
Do we remove the green slimy surface that forms on paths and terraces in winter especially in shady areas? It's slippery!

15. STEPS
Are all steps securely constructed?
Are loose or broken steps immediately repaired or blocked off from use?
Are the rises and treads on steps equal to avoid the risk of trips?
Are there handrails alongside if we have aged or handicapped persons in the family?

16. WALLS
Are retaining walls strong enough to support the infill behind, especially during and after heavy storms?
Are boundary walls on secure foundations, especially when you have heavy climbers growing on them?
Do walls have sufficient pipes to allow flood water to run away during storms?

17. FENCES
Are fence posts secure?
Are the fence sections or wire mesh secure?
Have climbing plants become top heavy?
Are supporting wires secure?

18. PONDS
Are ponds placed away from main paths and the edges secure?
Can ponds be easily fenced off or covered when young children are resident or visiting?
Are pond chemicals stored securely?

19. SWIMMING POOLS
Are swimming pool terraces made of non-slip slabs or tiles?
Do we check for sharp edges outside and within the pool regularly?
Are they speedily removed?
Is the pool fenced off to prevent unattended young children from using it or falling in?

Are the shallow end and depths clearly marked?
Are pool chemicals stored securely?
Have we changed to non-chemical cleaning methods?

20. BONFIRES
Do we avoid bonfires by using a skip instead?
If we have a bonfire do we obtain the necessary licence and follow local safety bylaws?
Do we have a safe burning area e.g. a bin or a brick screen?
Do we always stay with bonfires?
Do we ensure that we have a working hosepipe or buckets of water to avoid fires getting out of control?
Do we put out and dampen down the fire before leaving it?

21. LIFTING
Do we avoid lifting heavy rocks, sacks etc., without help?
Do we ensure that we do not overload the wheelbarrow?
Do we avoid mixing too much concrete at one time?

We hope that the above check list will help reduce the number of garden related accidents.

82. *Practical gardening tools*

Many gardening tools designed for northern European gardens are no match for traditional Spanish tools designed to cope with hard-baked Spanish soils and tall climbers we all plant in our new gardens. We soon found what was best to use by watching Spaniards at work, visiting agricultural cooperatives and trial and error. The mix of tools we now use are described below with a note on their uses, benefits and faults.

TOOLS BROUGHT FROM NORTHERN EUROPE

1. Scissors - still useful for cutting raffia and string.
2. Secateurs - which are universal, both short and long still essential.
3. Hedging shears - as always useful for tidying up shrubs, hedges and herbs.
4. Pliers - for cutting, training and tying wires.
5. Dutch hoe - use between plants, not as useful as double sided hoe. Leaves roots of deep rooted Spanish perennials.
6. Lawn rake - good for smartening up gravel and chipping paths and terraces.
7. Fork - we use both much less than before coming to Spain.
8. Spade - use largely in damp soil for digging up plants and vegetables and for planting, but in the hard soil they do not make much impact except on hands and backs. Handles broke but were easily replaced.
9. Small trowel and fork - use, but often replaced by small Spanish type 'mattock' with a short handle.

TRADITIONAL SPANISH TOOLS

10. Mattocks - a. *Small* - indispensable for hoeing, weeding, making seed drills and planting.
b. *Medium double ended* - a very useful tool used daily. Takes strain out of planting, heavy weeding, etc. Especially handy for ladies.
c. *Large* - major uses are digging holes and trenches, removing large roots.
b and *c* often come with handles that are ergonomically too short. Buy with long handle or buy blade and handle separately to suit your height.
11. Heavy ridging rake - with its long handle makes light work of preparing seed beds and constructing building and irrigation waterways.
12. Long extendible pruners - indispensable for cutting back high climbers and the higher smaller branches of trees.
13. Short and long handled pruning saws - Essential for pruning palms, cacti and trees. An extendible pole is especially useful.
14. Brooms - a heavy bristle broom and traditional Spanish garden broom will cover all jobs.
15. Black plastic buckets, as used by Spanish builders and gardeners - extremely useful for holding a plastic sack when weeding and pruning. Also for moving earth, manure, etc. Use in combination with a wheelbarrow for heavy loads. Available in various shapes and sizes.
16. Woven baskets - locally made baskets for collecting and storing vegetables.

MODERN MULTITOOLS

There are several makes available with a standard handle and a multitude of attachments.

We find that the most useful heads are -

1. THE DOUBLE-SIDED HOE - useful for cutting off annual weeds in hot weather when the ground is rock hard, loosening soil on the surface only. If soil is damp it is easier to work over.

2. THE THREE PRONGED HARROW - works well if the soil is damp or too wet to use the hoe. Also useful for covering large seeds after planting.

3 THE FLEXIBLE METAL RAKE - useful for clearing leaves from under shrubs. There is a narrow one with a short handle for flower beds.

Naturally an electric hedge cutter, suction blower and shredder can be useful, depending on the design of your garden.

We hope this review of tools helps you take some of the toil and strain out of gardening. It may lead to some useful birthday and Christmas presents.

83. *Establishing a compost heap*

All gardens benefit from a compost heap. They are easy to build and can be hidden away in a corner of the garden. A compost heap has several benefits.
1. The creation of your own compost for planting seeds and plants and for mulching.
2. The compost heap produces compost by biodegradation of kitchen and garden waste and therefore costs little.
3. Your daily rubbish will be reduced.
4. You will have less need for polluting bonfires.

The compost heap can simply be a pile of rubbish. However, it is preferable to have a definite container of minimum size one cubic metre. Two containers are better than one. The first can be decomposing while the second is filled. A practical composter can be created by four posts surrounded by wire netting or three block walls with a wire or wooden closure on the front side. There are also proprietary plastic compost bins or rotating composter. These are obviously more expensive.

Before filling your chosen compost container consider the necessary ingredients for good reliable rich compost.
There are seven main ingredients, as follows:
1. Green materials - these include kitchen waste from vegetables and fruit, non-meat food scraps, soft green cuttings and prunings, nitrogen rich grass cuttings (but not after weedkilling), torn up wetted newspaper or cardboard and annual garden weeds. Add leaves of perennial weeds such as dandelions, but not large tap roots.
2. Brown materials include dry fibrous materials such as shredded hard prunings, branches and cuttings, flower heads and stalks, dry leaves etc.
3. The optimum mix is 50 per cent green, 50 per cent brown materials. If you have insufficient green material add a compost activator. This could be comfrey leaves, nettle leaves, a strawless manure (preferably poultry), sulphate of ammonia or a proprietary powder. These will stimulate the growth of the necessary bacteria in the heap.
4. If you have too much green material add more brown material. Straw or dried ferns can be used.
5. Wood ash if you have it. This will add valuable potassium and lime.
6. Garden worms. These will be attracted to the heap from the surrounding garden. However, if you dig any up add them to the compost heap to speed the process.
7. Water: Composting materials need to be kept moist (but not wringing wet) for the bacteria and fungi essential to the decomposition process to grow rapidly and build up heat.

Load your compost container with alternative 10-15cm layers of brown and green materials, damp each layer in turn. Cover with cardboard, plastic or a piece of carpet to keep out heavy rain and to retain the heat and moisture.

During the summer you should have a good compost within three months. In the cooler winter, the process may take six months. The process will be faster if the composting materials are turned over regularly and slower if you leave an untouched heap. A correctly operated compost heap should create few problems.

If the following problems occur, the solutions are simple.
1. The process is slow to start. Turn the heap over with a fork. If too dry add more moisture and composting accelerator.
2. The final compost is too acid. The optimum pH is 6.0-7.0 for most vegetables and flowers. Turn over the heap and add lime. Next year add a sprinkling of lime every 25cms or every two layers of the heap.
3. The heap attracts rodents. Don't add meat scraps, fat or oil to the heap. In the short term set a trap or bait ensuring that pets cannot get near.
4. The heap becomes too wet. The result will be a slimy, foul smelling material. If this occurs open up the heap and add more dry materials. Turn the heap weekly until it smells sweet. Then cover and leave for the regular process to develop.
5. The heap attracts fruit flies. Turn over and add dry leaves or grass.

If you collect excess dry brown materials stack some in a pile ready to mix in at a later date. The pile will also attract useful hibernating wildlife, such as the hedgehog and toad.

The compost will be ready when a handful crumbles easily, is dark brown, pleasant to handle and has no unpleasant smell.

For potting seeds or plants mix the raw compost with fine soil and sand. A 1:1:1 mix will be useful for most purposes. For mulching use the raw compost in a 5-10cm layer. This will retain moisture and stimulate the growth of healthy plants. In turn the latter will reduce the need for chemical fertilisers and pesticides.

84. *Bonfires*

Sometimes a helicopter view of parts of the Costas could suggest that we are back in the ages of charcoal burners, and every household cooking on a wood fire. In reality the fires are burning rubbish dumps, fires in the fruit orchards and winter garden bonfires. The latter may be required from time to time to burn diseased plants, the only safe and rapid way to destroy them. But in general bonfires can be limited especially if you have an interest in organic gardening.

The following guidelines are therefore recommended.
1. See the bonfire as the last resort. The burning of vegetable material destroys useful nutrients that can be better recycled back into the soil.
2. Instead -
- put all soft cuttings and weeds on the compost heap. If you don't have a compost heap check whether a neighbour would like your material to add to theirs. Woody cuttings are easy to shred if done shortly after cutting and an excellent material for the compost heap or for mulching.
- send material to the local dump via the special containers provided in some areas or by personal delivery.

3. If you decide to have a bonfire, take the following precautions.
a. check on the local by-laws regarding the possibility of having a bonfire, the months they are allowed and which days of the week.

b. obtain an official licence from the local town hall.

c. before lighting the bonfire, make sure that you have a

hosepipe nearby and that there is a water supply.

d. only light a bonfire on a calm day and preferably early morning. On a windy day sparks can create a fire risk to your own garden as well as neighbouring properties.

e. to help control the fire, do your burning within an old drum or a brick-built fire screen as often seen around the orange fields. This will not only contain the fire but also achieve the temperature necessary for a fire rather than a smouldering heap and excessive smoke.

f. only put on vegetable matter. Don't be tempted to burn old plastic sacks, flower pots etc. The National Geographic Magazine reported in October that rural barrel bonfires in the USA release as many dangerous dioxins as did all the municipal incinerators combined. It is a hazard that gardeners can help reduce.

g. avoid a fire at the weekend. Working Spaniards along the road are probably planning a paella party or the weekly wash.

h. most importantly, once lit stay with the fire. When burnt out hose down the final ashes and surrounding area.

i. check an hour later that nothing has started to smoulder or burn as a result of fanning by the wind.

j. the final wood ash is a source of potassium. Sieve it and mix with the compost heap. Keep what you can't use immediately in a dry place. You can also make a line around seedlings to act as a slug barrier. However, this is not totally effective and will only work while the ash is dry.

k. it is best not to add wood ash to the soil. It dissolves very quickly and can make some soils slimy.

85. *Twenty jobs for a rainy day*

When autumn arrives, hopefully we will get a few wet days, even if the 'gota fria' doesn't come. A wet day is a chance to catch up on some of the many gardening jobs that can be done inside. We suggest the following 20 jobs as thought starters, knowing that it will take most of us several years to get them all done!

1. Review and improve the garden design.
2. Visit indoor garden centres for ideas.
3. Read gardening books and magazines for ideas.
4. Clean and repaint/revarnish garden furniture.
5. Paint decorative flower pots.
6. Make seed trays.
7. Make the sections for a frame for bringing on seeds and plants.
8. Clean up and repair garden tools, e.g. straighten up the prongs on the fork and fit new handles to the broom and rake.
9. Prepare a crop rotation and planting plan for the vegetable garden.
10. Refine the plan by reference to a lunar calendar and companion planting chart.
11. Prepare a seed list and send off for catalogues.
12. Sort seeds you have into planting date order.
13. Make seed and plant labels.
14. Update and review last season's vegetable garden records.
15. Make a list of garden plants, shrubs and trees for autumn planting and decide where to search/buy.
16. Make vegetable storage boxes.
17. Make covers for tender seeds and plants.
18. Sort through stored vegetables.
19. Review stock of herbicides, insecticides and fertilisers if used. Decide whether to change to organic gardening. If not prepare buying list.
20. Prepare a materials list for building new walls, terraces etc.
21. Have a rest from gardening!

Hopefully we won't have sufficient wet days to complete the list as the autumn is a good time for planting new shrubs and trees.

On reflection one more job should be added. We have some exceptionally dry summers. A rainy day is therefore a good time to design and start to construct a system for utilising the grey water from the kitchen sink, washing machine and showers for watering the garden.
The following is suggested as a basic process.

[Diagram: Sink, Shower, Washing m/c feeding into Sieve tank (Sediment), then tank with Rocks collect grease, then final tank with Final sediment, and Hose to garden]

The series of three tanks should separate out solids, oils and fats and ensure that the water is cool before reaching plants. The tanks do not need to be large, 100 litres each should suffice. Once installed you can move the exit hose to a different part of the garden daily. The system will also be a convenient means of fertilising the garden. Add liquid fertiliser, preferably organic to the final tank at regular intervals during the growing season.

86. Garden planting chart   Year:

Plant	Variety	Seed or Plant	Source	Key Dates				Yields if fruit or vegetable	General observations - feeds - sprays, etc.
				Planted	Transplanted	Flowered	Fruited	Harvested		

87. Garden expenditure chart   Year:

Date	Bill No.	Item purchased	Where from	Cost	Cost Analysis							
					Seeds	Compost	Containers	Fertilizers	Water	Herbicides/Pesticides	Canes/Posts/Wire/String	Other

Total Expenditures

88. Word corner

The word corner includes a selected vocabulary useful to the gardener. It is split into several sections.

A. The garden - El jardín
B. Parts of plants - Partes de plantas
C. Tools - Herramientas
D. Useful verbs - Verbos útiles
E. Plant names - Nombres de plantas

A. THE GARDEN - EL JARDÍN

annual - un anual
aromatic plant - una planta aromática
autumn - el otoño
blossom - las flores
bonfire - una hoguera
bulb - un bulbo
climber - una trepadora
compost heap - un montón de abono vegetal
fence - una cerca
fertilizer - el abono
flower - una flor
flower bed - un arriate/un cuadro
flower pot - una maceta
fruit - una fruta
garden - el jardín
gardener - el jardinero
ground cover plant - un progresivo
fungicide - un fungicida
hedge - un seto
herbicide - la herbicida
lawn - el césped
manure - el estiércol
mulch - el mantillo
orchard - un huerto
organic/ecological - ecologico
path - una vereda

perennial - perenne
pesticide - un pesticida
plant - una planta
pollen - el polen
pond - un estanque
rain - la lluvia
rambler - una enredadera
rockery - un jardincito
seat - la silla
seed - una semilla
seedbox - una caja de simientes
seedhead - una cabezuela
seed drill - la sembradora
scent - el olor
shade - la sombra
shrub - un arbusto
spring - la primavera
summer - el verano
sun - el sol
table - una mesa
sun umbrella - un parasol
vegetable - una verdura, una legumbre
vegetable plot - una huerta
wall - un muro
watering system - un sistema de riego
weed - una mala hierba
wild life - la fauna
winter - el invierno

B. PARTS OF PLANTS - PARTES DE PLANTAS

branch - una rama
bud (flower) - un capullo
bud (leaf) - una yema
cutting - un esqueje
flower - una flor
flower head - una cabezuela
leaf - una hoja
plant - una planta
root - una raiz
seed - una semilla
stem - un tallo
trunk - un tronco

C. TOOLS - HERRAMIENTAS

axe - el hacha *(fem.)*
broom - la escoba
fork - la horca
garden frame - una cajonera, una cama fria
greenhouse - un invernadero
hammer - el martillo
harrow - la grada
hoe - la azada
hosepipe - la manguera

mattock - el azadón
plough - el arado
rake - el rastrillo
saw - la sierra
secateurs - las tijeras de podar
sieve - una criba
spade - una pala
trowel - el desplantador
watering can - la regadera
wheelbarrow - la carretilla

D. USEFUL VERBS - VERBOS ÚTILES

attract - atraer
burn - quemar
cascade - caer en cascada
clear away - quitar
clean up - limpiar
cover up - cubrir
cut - cortar
cut back - recortar
cut down - talar
dehead - descabezar
dig (general) - cavar
dig (a hole) - excavar
dig in - añadir
divide - dividir
fertilize - fertilizar
gather/harvest - recoger
harrow - gradar
hoe - azadonar
maximise - maximizar
minimise - minimizar
mow - cortar
pinch off - quitar con los dedos
plant (plant) - plantar
plant (seeds) - sembrar
plough - arar
plough in - cubrir arando
propagate - propagar
protect - proteger
prune - podar
purchase - comprar
raise plants - producir
rake - rastrillar

rotavate - trabajar con motocultor
screen off - tapar
select - escoger
shade - proteger del sol/de la luz
shelter - resguardar
sow - sembrar
spray - pulverizar
stake (a tree) - rodrigar
stimulate - estimular
survive - sobrevivir
sweep - barrer
thin out - entresacar
tidy up - arreglar
tie up - atar
top up - llenar
transplant - transplantar
trench - excavar
water - regar
weed - desherbar

E. NAMES OF POPULAR PLANTS - NOMBRES DE PLANTAS POPULARES

Annuals, biennials and perennials
Anuales, bianuales y perennes

alstroemeria - alstroemeria
antirrhinum - antirrino
bird of paradise (strelitzia) - estralicia
busy lizzie - impatiens
cactus - cactus
carnation - clavel
chrysanthemum - crisantemo
cyclamen - ciclamen
dahlia - dalia
echium - echinium
elephants ear - oreja de elefante
gazania - gazania
geranium - geranio
hollyhock - malva
daisy - margarita
lupin - lupino
mesembryanthemum - mesembrianthemun
marigold - caléndula
nasturtium - capuchina
portulaca - verdolaga
pink - clavellina
pansy - pensamiento
petunia - petunia
poppy - amapola
rock roses - cistus
sedum - sedum
stock - alhelí
sunflower - girasol
san diego (flower of the night) - san diego de noche
sweet pea - guisante de olor
sage - salvia
sweet william - minutisa
valerian - valeriana
zinnia - zinnia

Vegetables and soft fruit - Verduras y frutas

artichoke - alcachofa
asparagus - espárrago
beans - judias
beetroot - remolacha
broad beans - habas
cabbage - col
carrot - zanahoria
courgette - calabacín
leek - puerro
lettuce - lechuga
melon - melón
parsnip - chirivia
onion - cebolla
pea - guisante
potatoes - patatas
pumpkin/squash - calabaza
radish - rábano
raspberry - frambuesa
spinach - espinaca
strawberry - fresa
swiss chard - acelga
tomato - tomate

Shrubs - Arbustos

bay - laurel
camelia - camelia
broom - hiniesta
bougainvillea - buganvilla
buddleia - buddleia
bottlebrush - callistemon
ceonothus - chaquira
datura - dativia
devil's tongue - lengua de diablo
fuchsia - fucsia
hibiscus - hibisco
hydrangea - hortensia
lantana - lantana
lavatera - malvia
mock orange (philadelphus) - jeringuilla
oleander - adelfa
plumbago - celestina
poinsettia - flor de pascua, poinsettia
pyracanthia - espino de fuego
rock rose - cistus
rose - rosal
tamarisk - tamarisco
yucca - yuca

Climbing shrubs
Arbustos trepadores

bignonia - bignonia
bougainvillea - buganvilla
clematis - clemátide
honeysuckle - madreselva
ivy - hiedra
jasmine - jazmín
kiwi - kiwi
morning glory - campanillas
passion flower - pasionaria
rose - rosal
solandra - solandra
wisteria - wisteria

Bulbous plants
Plantas bulbosas

agapanthus - agapante
amaryllis - amarilis
anemone - anemone
arum lily cala
cyclamen - ciclamen
canna - caña
clivia - clivia
crocus - azafran
daffodil - narciso
freesia - fresia
ginger - jengibre
gladiolus - gladiolo
grape hyacinth - jacinto de penacho
hyacinth - jacinto
iris - lirio
lily - lirio
ranunculus - ranunculo
tulip - tulipan

Ornamental trees
Arboles ornamentales

powder puff tree - albizzia
cedar - cedro
eucalyptus - eucalipto
flower of the night - galán de noche
lagerstroemia - lagerstroemia
jacaranda - jacarandá
judas tree - arbol de amor
juniper - juniper
lawsonia - lawsoniana
magnolia - magnolia
mimosa - mimosa
oleander - adelfa
palm - palmera
pittsoporum - pittosporum
rubber tree - arbol de caucho
strawberry tree - arbutus
tamarisk - tamarisco

Culinary and aromatic herbs
Hierbas culinarias y aromáticas

anise - anís
basil - albahaca
borage - borraja
camomile - manzanilla
chive - cebollino
coriander - cilantro
dill - eneldo
fennel - hinojo
parsley - perejil
lavender - espliego, lavanda
marjoram - mejorana
oregano - orégano
rosemary - romero
rue - ruda
sage - salvia
thyme - tomillo
verbena - verbena

Fruit and nut trees
Arboles frutales

apple - manzano
almond - almendro
apricot - albaricoquero
avocado - aquacate
banana - platano
carob - algarrobo
cherry - cerezo
chestnut - castaño
fig - higuera
grapefruit - pomelo
grapevine - vid
hazelnut - avellano
lemon - limonero
mango - mango
loquat - nispero
oak - roble
olive - olivo
orange - naranjo
peach - melocotonero
pear - peral
pistachio - pistacho
plum - ciruelo
pomegranate - granado
quince - membrillo
walnut - nogal

89. Useful English-Spanish questions and possible answers

We list a number of useful questions from a gardener in three typical situations and what could be typical replies to help you cope in your early days in Spain

AT THE GARDEN CENTRE - En el vivero

1. Do you stock 'X'?	¿Tienen ustedes 'X'?	Sí, tenemos estas marcas.	Yes, we have these brands.
2. What is this plant called?	¿Cómo se llama esta planta?	Gazania.	Gazania.
3. What colour is the flower?	¿Esta planta, que color tiene?	Rosa.	Pink.
4. When is it in flower?	¿Cuándo florece esta planta?	Desde marzo hasta junio.	From March until June.
5. How large is the mature plant?	¿Cómo se hace esta planta de grande?	Puede tener una altura de dos metros y una anchura de dos metros y medio.	It can become two metres high and two and a half metres wide.
6. Does this plant need a lot of water?	¿Necesita mucha agua esta planta?	Sí, necesita mucha agua.	Yes, it needs a lot of water.
7. Is this plant best in the sun or in the shade?	¿A esta planta le va el sol o la sombra?	Prefiere el sol.	It prefers full sun.
8. What price is this?	¿Cuánto vale?	Doce euros.	Twelve euros.
9. What are your opening hours?	¿A que hora abren?	Desde las nueve hasta las ocho de la tarde.	From 9am until 8pm.
10. Do you deliver to Jávea?	¿Tiene servicio a domicilio en Jávea?	Sí, martes y jueves.	Yes, Tuesday and Thursday.

IN THE HORTICULTURAL SHOP OR AGRICULTURAL COOPERATIVE - En la tienda de horticultura o la cooperativa agricola

1. Do you have carrot seeds?	¿Tiene semillas de zanahoria?	Sí, tres variedades.	Yes, three varieties.
2. When do you plant them here?	¿Cuándo se siembra aquí?	Normalmente en marzo.	Normally in March.
3. Do you sell black plastic?	¿Tienen plástico negro?	Sí, ¿cuánto quieres?	Yes, how much do you want?
4. What width do you have?	¿De qué ancho tienen?	Tenemos de dos y de cuatro.	We have two and four.
5. Ten metres, please.	Diez metros por favor.	¿De cual?	Which one?
6. What tools do you have?	¿Qué herramientas tienen?	Una buena selección. Allí las tiene.	A good selection, they are over there.
7. This handle is too short. Do you have a longer one?	Este mango es demasiado corto. ¿Tienen uno mas largo?	Sí, hay tres largos.	Yes, there are three lengths.
8. Do you have a general fertiliser?	¿Tienen un abono que sirve para todo?	Sí, este es para las flores y las legumbres.	Yes, this is for flowers and vegetables.
9. I would like 20 two-metre-long canes.	Quiero veinte cañas de dos metros.	¿Natural o verde?	Natural or dyed green?
10. When do you sell tomato plants?	¿Cuando tendrán ustedes plantas de tomate?	Normalmente en marzo y abril	Generally in March and April.

WITH THE GARDENER - Con el jardinero

1. Can you look after our garden?	¿Puede usted cuidar nuestro jardín?	Sí.	Yes.
2. How much will it cost?	¿Cuánto me costaría?	Ciento ochenta euros por mes.	180 euros a month.
3. For how many hours is that?	¿Por cuántas horas?	Dos o tres horas por semana, depende de la epoca.	Two or three hours a week depending on the time of year.
4. Can you plant more herbs?	¿Puede plantar mas hierbas aromáticas?	Sí, ¿pero dónde?	Yes, but where would you like them?
5. Can we reduce the size of the lawn?	¿Podemos reducir el tamaño del césped?	No es problema.	That's no problem.
6. When do you prune shrubs?	¿Cuándo se podan los arbustos?	Normalmente en enero.	Normally in January.
7. When can we plant bulbs?	¿Cuándo podemos plantar bulbos?	Es mejor en octubre y noviembre.	It's best in October and November.
8. Is this plant dead?	¿Está esta planta muerta?	No, está invernando.	No, it is dormant.
9. Can you cut the lawn today?	¿Puede cortar el césped hoy?	No, lo cortaré mañana por la mañana.	No, I will be cutting it tomorrow morning.
10. May we have the bill?	¿Nos puede dar la cuenta?	Si, lo tengo en el coche. Un momento.	Yes, I have it in the car. One moment.

90. *Requests for help*

Requests for help are welcomed for the weekly column of Practical Gardening by Greenfingers in Costa Blanca News and Costa del Sol News. Your problems will be dealt with in an appropriate column. Please use the following format when sending in requests.
We suggest that you cut out, photostat or copy the page onto your computer as appropriate.

To   GREENFINGERS
            C/O COSTA BLANCA NEWS

Via one of the following addresses
            EMAIL.   - cbn@costablancanews.es
            FAX: - 96 585 83 61
            POSTAL: - Apartado 95
                              03500 Benidorm
                              (Alicante)

From   Name:
            Address:

            Tel/Fax:
            Email: Date:

REQUEST
Please help me with the following gardening problem or information. I recognise that any advice given to me will be incorporated in a future weekly 'Practical Gardening by Greenfingers' in Costa Blanca News and Costa del Sol News and that my name will be mentioned.

....
....
....

AUTHORS' ACKNOWLEDGEMENTS

Having completed the enjoyable task of compiling Practical Gardening on the Costa we wish to give public recognition to the following persons who helped enrich our gardening experience and facilitate the publication of this book.

- To friends, clients and neighbours who have shared experience, listened to advice and provided opportunities for our continuous practical experimentation and learning.
- To those readers of our weekly column in CBN and CDSN who sent in interesting questions which broadened the topics covered in the book.
- To parents and grandparents for stimulating an early and ongoing interest in gardening.
- To Spain for providing the climate in which we enjoy our gardening.
- To Chelo and Alfonso Donet who kindly loan their ancient terrace for our organic vegetable garden.
- To each other for stimulating a continuous and challenging evolution of our gardens and gardening practice.
- To Theresa Marín for designing the book.
- To Artes Gráficas Esquerdo for their skill in producing an eyecatching book.
- To Peter Baker and Manuel Garay of CB News S.L. for sponsoring the book and accepting the practical A4 size.
- To each and all, our grateful thanks. Without you the book would not have been produced to help the betterment of expatriate gardening.

Practical Gardening on the Costa
Personal notes for action

Practical Gardening on the Costa
Personal notes for action

Practical Gardening on the Costa
Personal notes for action

Index

A

Absentee gardener	9
Absentee challenge	9
Aloes	37
Almonds	6, 35, 74
Animals	39, 41, 43
Annuals	13, 16, 27, 30
Aphids	28, 32, 52, 55, 59, 67, 76
Asparagus	50, 66
Autumn clean up	
flower garden	15, 16
vegetable garden	52, 53
Autumn propagation	17
Azaleas	47, 48

B

Birds	39
Bignonia	11, 24
Black fly	13, 33, 49, 55
Bonfires	84
Bougainvillea	11, 15, 24
Brassicas	67
Broad beans	49, 53
Broccoli	51, 67
Brussels sprouts	51, 67
Bulbs	30, 42
Busy lizzies	26
Butterflies	40, 41, 67

C

Cabbage	51, 67
Cacti	3, 37
Cacti - Christmas	16, 47, 48
Calendar, flower garden	
Jan/Feb	11
Mar/Apr	12
May/Jun	13
Jul/Aug	14
Sept/Oct	15
Nov/Dec	16
Calendar, vegetable garden	
Feb/Mar	49
Apr/May	50
Jun/Jul	51
Aug/Sep	52
Oct/Nov	53
Dec/Jan	54
Calendar - lunar	54, 59
Camelias	34
Canes	49, 71
Carobs	74
Carrots	50, 51
Cash crop trees	74
Cauliflower	51, 67
Challenge	
- Spanish gardening	1
Children's corner	8
Christmas plants	47, 48
Citrus fruits	73
Citrus trees	73

Clean up, flower garden	
winter	11
spring	12
autumn	15
Climbing plants	24
Clothing, protective	81
Colour matching	25
Comfrey, Russian	56, 76
Companion planting	32, 58, 59
Compost heap	13, 83
Corner	
children's	8
cosy	6
Courgettes	65
Crop rotation	51, 60
Cuttings, propagation	17, 33
Cyclamen	47, 48

D

Decoction, herbs	76
Design	
garden	2, 3, 4, 5
elderly/disabled	10
Disabled - design for	10
Driveway	7

E

Earthworms	53, 57, 58
Ecological system	57, 58
Ecological solutions	76, 81
Elderly, design for	10
Electricity	81
Exotic plants, from seed	13
Expenditure record	87

F

Feeds, natural	50, 51, 52, 76
Fire risks	7, 84
Fish	44
Flower garden	
Jan/Feb	11
Mar/Apr	12
May/Jun	13
Jul/Aug	14
Sep/Oct	15
Nov/Dec	16
Flowering times	
plants	9
trees	35
Fragrance	30
Fruit	
citrus	73
orchard	70
soft	71
Fruit trees, pruning	75
Fuchsias	26
Furniture	46

G

Galan de noche	11
Garden	
absentee	9
challenge	1
children's	8
established	2
frame	80
furniture	46
herb	29
in pines	7
improvement priorities	2
new	3
natural	39
organic	57
ornaments	46
overgrown	4
perfume	30
pond	43, 44
review	2
safety	81
shade	3, 6
small	5
vegetable	49-68
Garlic	64, 76
Gazanias	18
Geraniums	19
Gourds	65
Grapefruit	73
Grapevines	17, 72
Greenfly	33
Greenhouse	80

H

Hedges	3, 5, 11, 38
Herb garden	3, 4, 11, 29, 30
Herbs, beneficial properties	29
Hollyhocks	13
Horsetail	8, 14, 17, 29, 50, 55, 76

I

Infusion, herbs	29, 76
Insecticides, natural	76

J

Jacaranda	9
Jasmine	4, 11
Jobs, rainy day	85

L

Lantanas	11, 20
Lawn	
avoid	9, 77
care	14
Leeks	51, 64
Lemon	73
Lettuce	50, 52
Lilies	30, 42
Lime	51, 61
Lunar calendar	54, 59

M

Margaritas	4, 14, 15
Marrows	65
Melons	69
Mint	29
Moon quarters, planting by	59

Moth	12, 13, 14, 15, 19, 76
Morning glory	24
Mulching, flowers	13
Multitools	82
Mushrooms	7

N

Natural feeds	50, 51, 52, 76
Neem	12, 13, 16, 55, 67, 73, 76
Nettle, feed	76
Nitrogen	61

O

Oleanders	11, 21
Olives	9, 74, 75
Onions	51, 64
Onion fly	64
Orange	73
Orchard	70
Organic gardening	52, 58

P

Palms	4, 11, 36
Peas	53
Perfume	30
Perennials	
planting	16
propagation	17
Petunias	26
Phosphate	61
Pine trees	7
Plant, protection	
flowers	13
fruit trees	55
vegetables	55
soft fruit	71
Plants	
annuals	13, 16, 27
climbing	24
colour matching	25
exotic	13
perennials	17
pond	44
spectacular	23
Planting plan	59, 86
Plastic bottles, use of	67, 78
Ploughing	53
Plumbago	4, 5, 9, 11
Poinsettia	23, 47, 48
Potash	61
Potassium soap	76
Potatoes	22, 49, 52
Ponds	7, 10, 39, 43, 44, 81
Pots, terrace	22
Prize vegetables	51
Propagation, cuttings (also under plant names)	15, 17, 33, 37
Pruning, flowers	
spring	12, 13
summer	14
autumn	15, 16
winter	11
Pruning, citrus trees	73
Pruning, fruit trees	75
Pruning, grapevines	72
Pruning, roses	32, 33
Pumpkin	65

R

Rainy day, jobs	85
Raspberries	71
Review	
flower garden	2
vegetable garden	58
Risks, garden	81
Risks, pine trees	7
Rockery	45
Roses	
mature	33
planting and care	11, 32
propagation	33
selection	31
Rules, basic design	1

S

Safety	81
San Pedro	15
Seaweed	49, 66
Seeds, keeping	14, 15
Shade	3, 6
Shredder	4, 11
Shrubs	16
Site plan	3
Site survey	3
Snails	55, 62
Soil	
improvement	61
testing	61
Spaghetti	68
Spectacular plants	23
Sprays, natural	76
Spring	
clean	12
plantings	12
Squashes	65
Storing vegetabes	52
Strawberries	71
Succulents	9, 22
Sulphur	65, 72
Sunflowers	39
Sweet peas	28

T

Terrace, pots	22
Terraces	
shady	6
size	6, 9
surfaces	5
where	3
Testing soil	61
Tomatoes	63
Tomato leaves, rust spray	76
Tools	12, 81, 82
Trees	
autumn planting	16
cash crop	74
citrus	73
flowering	35
orchard	70

V

Vegetable garden	
Feb/Mar	49
Apr/May	50
June/July	51
Aug/Sept	52
Oct/Nov	53
Dec/Jan	54
Vegetable garden, starting	49, 52, 53
Vocabulary - English/Spanish	88

W

Water	
grey	79
retention	78
Water crystals	78
Watering system	79
Waterless gardening	77
Water lilies	39, 44
Water melons	69
Whitefly	55, 67
Wildlife garden	39
Winter clean up	11
Woodland glades	7
Word corner	88
Worms	39, 53, 57, 58

X

Xmas plants	
purchase	47
acclimatisation	47
care	48

Y

Yucca	4, 9

Z

Zinnias	27

N.B. Not all plant names are listed as they appear month by month and under groups of plants, e.g. annuals and climbing plants.